MznLnx

Missing Links Exam Preps

Exam Prep for

Management Fundamentals: Concepts, Applications, Skill Development

Lussier, 4th Edition

The MznLnx Exam Prep is your link from the texbook and lecture to your exams.
The MznLnx Exam Preps are unauthorized and comprehensive reviews of your textbooks.

All material provided by MznLnx and Rico Publications (c) 2010
Textbook publishers and textbook authors do not particpate in or contribute to these reviews.

MznLnx

Rico
Publications

Exam Prep for Management Fundamentals: Concepts, Applications, Skill Development
4th Edition
Lussier

Publisher: Raymond Houge
Assistant Editor: Michael Rouger
Text and Cover Designer: Lisa Buckner
Marketing Manager: Sara Swagger
Project Manager, Editorial Production: Jerry Emerson
Art Director: Vernon Lowerui

Product Manager: Dave Mason
Editorial Assitant: Rachel Guzmanji
Pedagogy: Debra Long
Cover Image: Jim Reed/Getty Images
Text and Cover Printer: City Printing, Inc.
Compositor: Media Mix, Inc.

(c) 2010 Rico Publications

ALL RIGHTS RESERVED. No part of this work covered by the copyright may be reproduced or used in any form or by an means--graphic, electronic, or mechanical, including photocopying, recording, taping, Web distribution, information storage, and retrieval systems, or in any other manner--without the written permission of the publisher.

For more information about our products, contact us at:

Dave.Mason@RicoPublications.com

For permission to use material from this text or product, submit a request online to:

Dave.Mason@RicoPublications.com

Printed in the United States
ISBN:

Contents

CHAPTER 1
Management and Entrepreneurship — 1

CHAPTER 2
The Global Environment: Culture, Ethics, and Social Responsibility — 14

CHAPTER 3
Creative Problem Solving and Decision Making — 28

CHAPTER 4
Strategic and Operational Planning — 39

CHAPTER 5
Organizing and Delegating Work — 48

CHAPTER 6
Managing Change: Innovation and Diversity — 53

CHAPTER 7
Human Resources Management — 63

CHAPTER 8
Organizational Behavior: Power, Politics, Conflict, and Stress — 78

CHAPTER 9
Leading with Influence — 86

CHAPTER 10
Communicating and Information Technology — 91

CHAPTER 11
Motivating for High Performance — 97

CHAPTER 12
Team Leadership — 102

CHAPTER 13
Control Systems: Financial and Human — 106

CHAPTER 14
Operations, Quality, and Productivity — 112

ANSWER KEY — 124

TO THE STUDENT

COMPREHENSIVE

The *MznLnx* Exam Prep series is designed to help you pass your exams. Editors at MznLnx review your textbooks and then prepare these practice exams to help you master the textbook material. Unlike study guides, workbooks, and practice tests provided by the texbook publisher and textbook authors, *MznLnx* gives you **all** of the material in each chapter in exam form, not just samples, so you can be sure to nail your exam.

MECHANICAL

The MznLnx Exam Prep series creates exams that will help you learn the subject matter as well as test you on your understanding. Each question is designed to help you master the concept. Just working through the exams, you gain an understanding of the subject--its a simple mechanical process that produces success.

INTEGRATED STUDY GUIDE AND REVIEW

MznLnx is not just a set of exams designed to test you, its also a comprehensive review of the subject content. Each exam question is also a review of the concept, making sure that you will get the answer correct without having to go to other sources of material. You learn as you go! Its the easiest way to pass an exam.

HUMOR

Studying can be tedious and dry. MznLnx's instructional design includes moderate humor within the exam questions on occassion, to break the tedium and revitalize the brain

Chapter 1. Management and Entrepreneurship

1. Maslow's _____ is a theory in psychology, proposed by Abraham Maslow in his 1943 paper A Theory of Human Motivation, which he subsequently extended to include his observations of humans' innate curiosity.

   Maslow's _____ is predetermined in order of importance. It is often depicted as a pyramid consisting of five levels: the lowest level is associated with physiological needs, while the uppermost level is associated with self-actualization needs, particularly those related to identity and purpose. Deficiency needs must be met first. Once these are met, seeking to satisfy growth needs drives personal growth. The higher needs in this hierarchy only come into focus when the lower needs in the pyramid are met.

   a. 1990 Clean Air Act
   b. Hierarchy of needs
   c. 33 Strategies of War
   d. 28-hour day

2. _____ is an increasingly broadening term with which an organization, or other human system describes the combination of traditionally administrative personnel functions with acquisition and application of skills, knowledge and experience, Employee Relations and resource planning at various levels. The field draws upon concepts developed in Industrial/Organizational Psychology and System Theory. _____ has at least two related interpretations depending on context. The original usage derives from political economy and economics, where it was traditionally called labor, one of four factors of production although this perspective is changing as a function of new and ongoing research into more strategic approaches at national levels. This first usage is used more in terms of '_____ development', and can go beyond just organizations to the level of nations . The more traditional usage within corporations and businesses refers to the individuals within a firm or agency, and to the portion of the organization that deals with hiring, firing, training, and other personnel issues, typically referred to as `_____ management'.
   a. Bradford Factor
   b. Progressive discipline
   c. Human resources
   d. Human resource management

3. '_____' refers to mental and communicative algorithms applied during social communications and interactions in order to reach certain effects or results. The term '_____' is used often in business contexts to refer to the measure of a person's ability to operate within business organizations through social communication and interactions. _____ are how people relate to one another.
   a. A Stake in the Outcome
   b. AAAI
   c. A4e
   d. Interpersonal skills

4. _____ is the ability to visualize, articulate, and solve complex problems and concepts, and make decisions that make sense based on available information. Such skills include demonstration of the ability to apply logical thinking to gathering and analyzing information, designing and testing solutions to problems, and formulating plans.

Chapter 1. Management and Entrepreneurship

To test for _____s one might be asked to look for inconsistencies in an advertisement, put a series of events in the proper order, or critically read an essay.

   a. Analytical skill
   b. AAAI
   c. A Stake in the Outcome
   d. A4e

5. _____ is purposeful and reflective judgment about what to believe or what to do in response to observations, experience, verbal or written expressions, or arguments. _____ might involve determining the meaning and significance of what is observed or expressed, or, concerning a given inference or argument, determining whether there is adequate justification to accept the conclusion as true. Hence, Fisher ' Scriven define _____ as 'Skilled, active, interpretation and evaluation of observations, communications, information, and argumentation.' Parker ' Moore define it more narrowly as the careful, deliberate determination of whether one should accept, reject, or suspend judgment about a claim and the degree of confidence with which one accepts or rejects it.

   a. Virtual team
   b. Risk management
   c. Kanban
   d. Critical thinking

6. The 'business case for _____', theorizes that in a global marketplace, a company that employs a diverse workforce (both men and women, people of many generations, people from ethnically and racially diverse backgrounds etc.) is better able to understand the demographics of the marketplace it serves and is thus better equipped to thrive in that marketplace than a company that has a more limited range of employee demographics.

An additional corollary suggests that a company that supports the _____ of its workforce can also improve employee satisfaction, productivity and retention.

   a. Trademark
   b. Diversity
   c. Kanban
   d. Virtual team

7. A _____ is a list of the general tasks and responsibilities of a position. Typically, it also includes to whom the position reports, specifications such as the qualifications needed by the person in the job, salary range for the position, etc. A _____ is usually developed by conducting a job analysis, which includes examining the tasks and sequences of tasks necessary to perform the job.

a. Recruitment
b. Job description
c. Recruitment advertising
d. Recruitment Process Insourcing

8. A _____ or chief executive is one of the highest-ranking corporate officer (executive) or administrator in charge of total management. An individual selected as President and _____ of a corporation, company, organization, or agency, reports to the board of directors. In internal communication and press releases, many companies capitalize the term and those of other high positions, even when they are not proper nouns.
   a. Chief executive officer
   b. Financial analyst
   c. Chief brand officer
   d. Purchasing manager

9. While _____ literally refers to a person responsible for the performance of duties involved in running an organization, the exact meaning of the role is variable, depending on the organization.

While there is no clear line between executive or principal and inferior officers, principal officers are high-level officials in the executive branch of U.S. government such as department heads of independent agencies. In Humphrey's Executor v. United States, 295 U.S. 602 (1935), the Court distinguished between _____s and quasi-legislative or quasi-judicial officers by stating that the former serve at the pleasure of the President and may be removed at his discretion.

   a. Easement
   b. Australian Fair Pay and Conditions Standard
   c. Unreported employment
   d. Executive officer

10. _____ is how top executives of business corporations are paid. This includes a basic salary, bonuses, shares, options and other company benefits. Over the past three decades, _____ has risen dramatically beyond the rising levels of an average worker's wage.
    a. Evidence-based management
    b. Executive compensation
    c. Association management company
    d. Anti-leadership

11. _____ for short is a descriptive term for certain executives in a business operation. It is also a formal title held by some business executives, most commonly in the hospitality industry.

A _____ has broad, overall responsibility for a business or organization. Whereas a manager may be responsible for one functional area, the _____ is responsible for all areas.

a. Chief knowledge officer
b. Chief technology officer
c. Managing director
d. General manager

12. _____ is an integrated communications-based process through which individuals and communities discover that existing and newly-identified needs and wants may be satisfied by the products and services of others.

_____ is defined by the American _____ Association as the activity, set of institutions, and processes for creating, communicating, delivering, and exchanging offerings that have value for customers, clients, partners, and society at large. The term developed from the original meaning which referred literally to going to market, as in shopping, or going to a market to buy or sell goods or services.

a. Market development
b. Customer relationship management
c. Disruptive technology
d. Marketing

13. _____ refers to the movement of cash into or out of a business or financial product. It is usually measured during a specified, finite period of time. Measurement of _____ can be used

- to determine a project's rate of return or value. The time of _____s into and out of projects are used as inputs in financial models such as internal rate of return, and net present value.
- to determine problems with a business's liquidity. Being profitable does not necessarily mean being liquid. A company can fail because of a shortage of cash, even while profitable.
- as an alternate measure of a business's profits when it is believed that accrual accounting concepts do not represent economic realities. For example, a company may be notionally profitable but generating little operational cash (as may be the case for a company that barters its products rather than selling for cash.) In such a case, the company may be deriving additional operating cash by issuing shares evaluating default risk, re-investment requirements, etc.

_____ is a generic term used differently depending on the context. It may be defined by users for their own purposes.

a. Gross profit
b. Sweat equity
c. Gross profit margin
d. Cash flow

14. A _____ is a professional in the field of project management. _____s can have the responsibility of the planning, execution, and closing of any project, typically relating to construction industry, architecture, computer networking, telecommunications or software development.

Many other fields in the production, design and service industries also have _____s.

a. Project manager
b. Project management
c. Work package
d. Project engineer

15. _____ refers to the process of grouping activities into departments.

Division of labour creates specialists who need coordination. This coordination is facilitated by grouping specialists together in departments.

a. Maximum wage
b. Decent work
c. Departmentalization
d. Division of labour

16. _____ comprises a range of practices used in an organisation to identify, create, represent, distribute and enable adoption of insights and experiences. Such insights and experiences comprise knowledge, either embodied in individuals or embedded in organisational processes or practice.

An established discipline since 1991, _____ includes courses taught in the fields of business administration, information systems, management, and library and information sciences.

a. 33 Strategies of War
b. 28-hour day
c. 1990 Clean Air Act
d. Knowledge management

Chapter 1. Management and Entrepreneurship

17. A _____ is the term given to a company that facilitates the learning of its members and continuously transforms itself. _____s develop as a result of the pressures facing modern organizations and enables them to remain competitive in the business environment. A _____ has five main features; systems thinking, personal mastery, mental models, shared vision and team learning.
   a. Learning organization
   b. Quality function deployment
   c. 1990 Clean Air Act
   d. Hoshin Kanri

18. In probability theory, a probability distribution is called _____ if its cumulative distribution function is _____. This is equivalent to saying that for random variables X with the distribution in question, Pr[X = a] = 0 for all real numbers a, i.e.: the probability that X attains the value a is zero, for any number a. If the distribution of X is _____ then X is called a _____ random variable.
   a. Connectionist expert systems
   b. Pay Band
   c. Decision tree pruning
   d. Continuous

19. _____ is a management process whereby delivery (customer valued) processes are constantly evaluated and improved in the light of their efficiency, effectiveness and flexibility.

Some see it as a meta process for most management systems (Business Process Management, Quality Management, Project Management). Deming saw it as part of the 'system' whereby feedback from the process and customer were evaluated against organisational goals.

   a. Critical Success Factor
   b. First-mover advantage
   c. Sole proprietorship
   d. Continuous Improvement Process

20. _____ according to Onuoha (2007) is the practice of starting new organizations or revitalizing mature organizations, particularly new businesses generally in response to identified opportunities. _____ is often a difficult undertaking, as a vast majority of new businesses fail. Entrepreneurial activities are substantially different depending on the type of organization that is being started.
   a. AAAI
   b. A4e
   c. A Stake in the Outcome
   d. Entrepreneurship

Chapter 1. Management and Entrepreneurship

21. An _____ is a person who has possession of an enterprise and assumes significant accountability for the inherent risks and the outcome. It is an ambitious leader who combines land, labor, and capital to create and market new goods or services. The term is a loanword from French and was first defined by the Irish economist Richard Cantillon.
   a. Entrepreneur
   b. AAAI
   c. A Stake in the Outcome
   d. A4e

22. In decision theory and estimation theory, the _____ of an estimator, $\hat{\theta}$, of an unknown parameter of the distribution, θ, is the expected value of the loss function

$$R(\theta, \hat{\theta}) = \mathbb{E}_\theta L(\theta, \hat{\theta}) = \int L(\theta, \hat{\theta}) \, dP_\theta.$$

where dP_θ is a probability measure parametrized by θ.

- For a scalar parameter θ and a quadratic loss function,

$$L(\theta, \hat{\theta}) = (\theta - \hat{\theta})^2$$

the _____ function becomes the mean squared error of the estimate,

$$R(\theta, \hat{\theta}) = E_\theta (\theta - \hat{\theta})^2$$

- In density estimation, the unknown parameter is probability density itself. The loss function is typically chosen to be a norm in an appropriate function space. For example, for L^2 norm,

$$L(f, \hat{f}) = \|f - \hat{f}\|_2^2$$

the _____ function becomes the mean integrated squared error

$$R(f, \hat{f}) = E \|f - \hat{f}\|^2$$

a. Linear model
b. Risk aversion
c. Risk
d. Financial modeling

23. A _____ is a business that is privately owned and operated, with a small number of employees and relatively low volume of sales. The legal definition of 'small' often varies by country and industry, but is generally under 100 employees in the United States and under 50 employees in the European Union. In comparison, the definition of mid-sized business by the number of employees is generally under 500 in the U.S. and 250 for the European Union.

a. Critical Success Factor
b. Golden Boot Compensation
c. Pre-determined overhead rate
d. Small Business

24. The _____ is a United States government agency that provides support to small businesses.

The mission of the _____ is 'to maintain and strengthen the nation's economy by enabling the establishment and viability of small businesses and by assisting in the economic recovery of communities after disasters.'

The _____ makes loans directly to businesses and acts as a guarantor on bank loans. In some circumstances it also makes loans to victims of natural disasters, works to get government procurement contracts for small businesses, and assists businesses with management, technical and training issues.

a. 28-hour day
b. Small Business Administration
c. 1990 Clean Air Act
d. 33 Strategies of War

25. _____ is, in very basic words, a position a firm occupies against its competitors.

According to Michael Porter, the three methods for creating a sustainable _____ are through:

1. Cost leadership

2. Differentiation

3. Focus (economics)

a. 1990 Clean Air Act
b. 28-hour day
c. Theory Z
d. Competitive advantage

26. _____ is the increase in the amount of the goods and services produced by an economy over time and is dependent on an increase in the creation of money. Growth is conventionally measured as the percent rate of increase in real gross domestic product, or real GDP. GDP is usually calculated in real terms, i.e. inflation-adjusted terms, in order to net out the effect of inflation on the price of the goods and services produced.
  a. A Stake in the Outcome
  b. AAAI
  c. A4e
  d. Economic growth

27. _____ is the advantage gained by the initial occupant of a market segment. This advantage may stem from the fact that the first entrant can gain control of resources that followers may not be able to match. Sometimes the first mover is not able to capitalise on its advantage, leaving the opportunity for another firm to gain second-mover advantage.
  a. Customer retention
  b. Horizontal integration
  c. First-mover advantage
  d. Business ecosystem

28. A _____ is a formal statement of a set of business goals, the reasons why they are believed attainable, and the plan for reaching those goals. It may also contain background information about the organization or team attempting to reach those goals.

The business goals may be defined for for-profit or for non-profit organizations.

  a. Crisis management
  b. Time management
  c. Distributed management
  d. Business plan

29. Consumer market research is a form of applied sociology that concentrates on understanding the behaviours, whims and preferences, of consumers in a market-based economy, and aims to understand the effects and comparative success of marketing campaigns. The field of consumer _____ as a statistical science was pioneered by Arthur Nielsen with the founding of the ACNielsen Company in 1923 .

Thus _____ is the systematic and objective identification, collection, analysis, and dissemination of information for the purpose of assisting management in decision making related to the identification and solution of problems and opportunities in marketing.

a. Market analysis
b. Marketing research process
c. Marketing research
d. 1990 Clean Air Act

30. A _____ is a relatively new executive level position at a corporation, company, organization typically reporting directly to the CEO or board of directors. The _____ is responsible for a brand's image, experience, and promise, and propagating it throughout all aspects of the company. The brand officer oversees marketing, advertising, design, public relations and customer service departments.

a. Purchasing manager
b. Director of communications
c. Chief brand officer
d. Chief executive officer

31. _____ is an advertisement in which a particular product specifically mentions a competitor by name for the express purpose of showing why the competitor is inferior to the product naming it.

This should not be confused with parody advertisements, where a fictional product is being advertised for the purpose of poking fun at the particular advertisement, nor should it be confused with the use of a coined brand name for the purpose of comparing the product without actually naming an actual competitor. ('Wikipedia tastes better and is less filling than the Encyclopedia Galactica.')

In the 1980s, during what has been referred to as the cola wars, soft-drink manufacturer Pepsi ran a series of advertisements where people, caught on hidden camera, in a blind taste test, chose Pepsi over rival Coca-Cola.

a. 33 Strategies of War
b. 1990 Clean Air Act
c. 28-hour day
d. Comparative advertising

32. A _____ is one of several ways of doing research whether it is social science related or even socially related. It is an intensive study of a single group, incident, or community.Other ways include experiments, surveys, multiple histories, and analysis of archival information .

Rather than using samples and following a rigid protocol to examine limited number of variables, _____ methods involve an in-depth, longitudinal examination of a single instance or event: a case.

a. Case study
b. Standard operating procedure
c. 1990 Clean Air Act
d. Longitudinal study

33. _____ refers to increasing the spiritual, political, social or economic strength of individuals and communities. It often involves the empowered developing confidence in their own capacities.

The term Human _____ covers a vast landscape of meanings, interpretations, definitions and disciplines ranging from psychology and philosophy to the highly commercialized Self-Help industry and Motivational sciences.

a. A Stake in the Outcome
b. AAAI
c. Empowerment
d. A4e

34. _____ is a theory of management that analyzes and synthesizes workflows, with the objective of improving labour productivity. The core ideas of the theory were developed by Frederick Winslow Taylor in the 1880s and 1890s, and were first published in his monographs, Shop Management and The Principles of _____ Taylor believed that decisions based upon tradition and rules of thumb should be replaced by precise procedures developed after careful study of an individual at work.

a. Scientific management
b. Master production schedule
c. Value engineering
d. Capacity planning

35. _____, widely known as F. W. Taylor, was an American mechanical engineer who sought to improve industrial efficiency. He is regarded as the father of scientific management, and was one of the first management consultants.

Taylor was one of the intellectual leaders of the Efficiency Movement and his ideas, broadly conceived, were highly influential in the Progressive Era.

a. Jonah Jacob Goldberg
b. Geoffrey Colvin
c. Douglas N. Daft
d. Frederick Winslow Taylor

36. A _____ is a type of bar chart that illustrates a project schedule. _____s illustrate the start and finish dates of the terminal elements and summary elements of a project. Terminal elements and summary elements comprise the work breakdown structure of the project.
   a. 28-hour day
   b. 1990 Clean Air Act
   c. 33 Strategies of War
   d. Gantt chart

37. The _____ is a form of reactivity whereby subjects improve an aspect of their behavior being experimentally measured simply in response to the fact that they are being studied, not in response to any particular experimental manipulation.

The term was coined in 1955 by Henry A. Landsberger when analyzing older experiments from 1924-1932 at the Hawthorne Works (outside Chicago.) Hawthorne Works had commissioned a study to see if its workers would become more productive in higher or lower levels of light.

   a. 28-hour day
   b. 1990 Clean Air Act
   c. Hawthorne effect
   d. 33 Strategies of War

38. _____ Movement refers to those researchers of organizational development who study the behavior of people in groups, in particular workplace groups. It originated in the 1920s' Hawthorne studies, which examined the effects of social relations, motivation and employee satisfaction on factory productivity. The movement viewed workers in terms of their psychology and fit with companies, rather than as interchangeable parts.
   a. Work design
   b. Hersey-Blanchard situational theory
   c. Participatory management
   d. Human relations

39. _____ refers to those researchers of organizational development who study the behavior of people in groups, in particular workplace groups. It originated in the 1920s' Hawthorne studies, which examined the effects of social relations, motivation and employee satisfaction on factory productivity. The movement viewed workers in terms of their psychology and fit with companies, rather than as interchangeable parts.
  a. Human relations movement
  b. Job satisfaction
  c. Job analysis
  d. Path-goal theory

40. _____, is the discipline of using scientific research-based principles, strategies, and other analytical methods, such as mathematical modeling to improve any organization's ability to enact rational, meaningful business management decisions.
  a. Trustee
  b. Management science
  c. Workflow
  d. Cross ownership

41. _____ is a class of behavioural theory that claims that there is no best way to organize a corporation, to lead a company, or to make decisions. Instead, the optimal course of action is contingent (dependant) upon the internal and external situation. Several contingency approaches were developed concurrently in the late 1960s.
  a. Capability management
  b. Distributed management
  c. Commercial management
  d. Contingency theory

42. _____ is an interdisciplinary field of science and the study of the nature of complex systems in nature, society, and science. More specifically, it is a framework by which one can analyze and/or describe any group of objects that work in concert to produce some result. This could be a single organism, any organization or society, or any electro-mechanical or informational artifact.
  a. Systems theory
  b. Systems thinking
  c. 28-hour day
  d. 1990 Clean Air Act

Chapter 2. The Global Environment: Culture, Ethics, and Social Responsibility

1. _____, commonly known as e-commerce, consists of the buying and selling of products or services over electronic systems such as the Internet and other computer networks. The amount of trade conducted electronically has grown extraordinarily with widespread Internet usage. The use of commerce is conducted in this way, spurring and drawing on innovations in electronic funds transfer, supply chain management, Internet marketing, online transaction processing, electronic data interchange (EDI), inventory management systems, and automated data collection systems.

   a. A Stake in the Outcome
   b. A4e
   c. Online shopping
   d. Electronic Commerce

2. _____ refers to training in different ways to improve overall performance. It takes advantage of the particular effectiveness of each training method, while at the same time attempting to neglect the shortcomings of that method by combining it with other methods that address its weaknesses.

   Cross training is employee-employer field means, training employees to do one another's work.

   a. Cross-training
   b. 1990 Clean Air Act
   c. 33 Strategies of War
   d. 28-hour day

3. _____ is an idea in the field of Organizational studies and management which describes the psychology, attitudes, experiences, beliefs and Values (personal and cultural values) of an organization. It has been defined as 'the specific collection of values and norms that are shared by people and groups in an organization and that control the way they interact with each other and with stakeholders outside the organization.'

   This definition continues to explain organizational values also known as 'beliefs and ideas about what kinds of goals members of an organization should pursue and ideas about the appropriate kinds or standards of behavior organizational members should use to achieve these goals. From organizational values develop organizational norms, guidelines or expectations that prescribe appropriate kinds of behavior by employees in particular situations and control the behavior of organizational members towards one another.'

   _____ is not the same as corporate culture.

   a. Union shop
   b. Organizational effectiveness
   c. Organizational culture
   d. Organizational development

Chapter 2. The Global Environment: Culture, Ethics, and Social Responsibility

4. _____ describes the situation when output from (or information about the result of) an event or phenomenon in the past will influence the same event/phenomenon in the present or future. When an event is part of a chain of cause-and-effect that forms a circuit or loop, then the event is said to 'feed back' into itself.

_____ is also a synonym for:

- _____ signal; the information about the initial event that is the basis for subsequent modification of the event.
- _____ loop; the causal path that leads from the initial generation of the _____ signal to the subsequent modification of the event.

_____ is a mechanism, process or signal that is looped back to control a system within itself. Such a loop is called a _____ loop.

   a. 1990 Clean Air Act
   b. Positive feedback
   c. Feedback
   d. Feedback loop

5. _____ refers to the process of grouping activities into departments.

Division of labour creates specialists who need coordination. This coordination is facilitated by grouping specialists together in departments.

   a. Departmentalization
   b. Maximum wage
   c. Division of labour
   d. Decent work

6. A chief executive officer (_____) or chief executive is one of the highest-ranking corporate officer (executive) or administrator in charge of total management. An individual selected as President and _____ of a corporation, company, organization, or agency, reports to the board of directors. In internal communication and press releases, many companies capitalize the term and those of other high positions, even when they are not proper nouns.
   a. CEO
   b. Portfolio manager
   c. Chief executive officer
   d. Director of communications

7. Procter is a surname, and may also refer to:

- Bryan Waller Procter (pseud. Barry Cornwall), English poet
- Goodwin Procter, American law firm
- _____, consumer products multinational

a. Master and Servant Acts
b. Strict liability
c. Downstream
d. Procter ' Gamble

8. A _____ is the term given to a company that facilitates the learning of its members and continuously transforms itself. _____s develop as a result of the pressures facing modern organizations and enables them to remain competitive in the business environment. A _____ has five main features; systems thinking, personal mastery, mental models, shared vision and team learning.
   a. Learning organization
   b. 1990 Clean Air Act
   c. Quality function deployment
   d. Hoshin Kanri

9. _____ is an advertisement in which a particular product specifically mentions a competitor by name for the express purpose of showing why the competitor is inferior to the product naming it.

This should not be confused with parody advertisements, where a fictional product is being advertised for the purpose of poking fun at the particular advertisement, nor should it be confused with the use of a coined brand name for the purpose of comparing the product without actually naming an actual competitor. ('Wikipedia tastes better and is less filling than the Encyclopedia Galactica.')

In the 1980s, during what has been referred to as the cola wars, soft-drink manufacturer Pepsi ran a series of advertisements where people, caught on hidden camera, in a blind taste test, chose Pepsi over rival Coca-Cola.

a. Comparative advertising
b. 33 Strategies of War
c. 1990 Clean Air Act
d. 28-hour day

10. A _____ is a body of elected or appointed members who jointly oversee the activities of a company or organization. The body sometimes has a different name, such as board of trustees, board of governors, board of managers, or executive board. It is often simply referred to as 'the board.'

Chapter 2. The Global Environment: Culture, Ethics, and Social Responsibility

A board's activities are determined by the powers, duties, and responsibilities delegated to it or conferred on it by an authority outside itself.

   a. Board of directors
   b. Competition law
   c. Foreign Corrupt Practices Act
   d. Clean Water Act

11. In economics, the people in the _____ are the suppliers of labor. The _____ is all the nonmilitary people who are employed or unemployed. In 2005, the worldwide _____ was over 3 billion people.
   a. Decent work
   b. Pink-collar worker
   c. Departmentalization
   d. Labor force

12. A mutual _____ or stockholder is an individual or company (including a corporation) that legally owns one or more shares of stock in a joint stock company. A company's _____s collectively own that company. Thus, the typical goal of such companies is to enhance _____ value.
   a. Shareholder
   b. 1990 Clean Air Act
   c. Stockholder
   d. Free riding

13. A _____ is a relatively new executive level position at a corporation, company, organization typically reporting directly to the CEO or board of directors. The _____ is responsible for a brand's image, experience, and promise, and propagating it throughout all aspects of the company. The brand officer oversees marketing, advertising, design, public relations and customer service departments.
   a. Chief brand officer
   b. Chief executive officer
   c. Purchasing manager
   d. Director of communications

Chapter 2. The Global Environment: Culture, Ethics, and Social Responsibility

14. The _____ is an agency of the United States Department of Health and Human Services and is responsible for regulating and supervising the safety of foods, dietary supplements, drugs, vaccines, biological medical products, blood products, medical devices, radiation-emitting devices, veterinary products, and cosmetics. The FDA also enforces section 361 of the Public Health Service Act and the associated regulations, including sanitation requirements on interstate travel as well as specific rules for control of disease on products ranging from pet turtles to semen donations for assisted reproductive medicine techniques.

The FDA is an agency within the United States Department of Health and Human Services responsible for protecting and promoting the nation's public health.

   a. 33 Strategies of War
   b. 1990 Clean Air Act
   c. Food and Drug Administration
   d. 28-hour day

15. _____ is a cross-disciplinary area concerned with protecting the safety, health and welfare of people engaged in work or employment. The goal of all _____ programs is to foster a work free safe environment. As a secondary effect, it may also protect co-workers, family members, employers, customers, suppliers, nearby communities, and other members of the public who are impacted by the workplace environment.
   a. AAAI
   b. Occupational Safety and Health
   c. A Stake in the Outcome
   d. A4e

16. The United States _____ is an agency of the United States Department of Labor. It was created by Congress under the Occupational Safety and Health Act, signed by President Richard M. Nixon, on December 29, 1970. Its mission is to prevent work-related injuries, illnesses, and deaths by issuing and enforcing rules (called standards) for workplace safety and health.
   a. Operant conditioning
   b. Unemployment insurance
   c. Opinion leadership
   d. Occupational Safety and Health Administration

17. In finance, the _____s between two currencies specifies how much one currency is worth in terms of the other. It is the value of a foreign nation's currency in terms of the home nation's currency. For example an _____ of 102 Japanese yen to the United States dollar means that JPY 102 is worth the same as USD 1.

a. A4e
b. AAAI
c. A Stake in the Outcome
d. Exchange rate

18. _____ was a writer, management consultant, and self-described 'social ecologist.' Widely considered to be 'the father of modern management,' his 39 books and countless scholarly and popular articles explored how humans are organized across all sectors of society--in business, government and the nonprofit world. His writings have predicted many of the major developments of the late twentieth century, including privatization and decentralization; the rise of Japan to economic world power; the decisive importance of marketing; and the emergence of the information society with its necessity of lifelong learning. In 1959, Drucker coined the term 'knowledge worker' and later in his life considered knowledge work productivity to be the next frontier of management.
   a. Chrissie Hynde
   b. Debora L. Spar
   c. Jacques Al-Salawat Nasruddin Nasser
   d. Peter Ferdinand Drucker

19. _____ in its literal sense is the process of transformation of local or regional phenomena into global ones. It can be described as a process by which the people of the world are unified into a single society and function together.

This process is a combination of economic, technological, sociocultural and political forces.

   a. Histogram
   b. Globalization
   c. Collaborative Planning, Forecasting and Replenishment
   d. Cost Management

20. The _____ is the difference between the monetary value of exports and imports of output in an economy over a certain period of time. It is the relationship between a nation's imports and exports. A favourable _____ is known as a trade surplus and consists of exporting more than is imported; an unfavourable _____ is known as a trade deficit or, informally, a trade gap.
   a. Value added
   b. Balance of trade
   c. Deregulation
   d. Minimum wage

Chapter 2. The Global Environment: Culture, Ethics, and Social Responsibility

21. _____ is a type of trade policy that allows traders to act and transact without interference from government. Thus, the policy permits trading partners mutual gains from trade, with goods and services produced according to the theory of comparative advantage.

Under a _____ policy, prices are a reflection of true supply and demand, and are the sole determinant of resource allocation.

  a. 28-hour day
  b. 1990 Clean Air Act
  c. 33 Strategies of War
  d. Free Trade

22. _____ is a designated group of countries that have agreed to eliminate tariffs, quotas and preferences on most (if not all) goods and services traded between them. It can be considered the second stage of economic integration. Countries choose this kind of economic integration form if their economical structures are complementary.
  a. 33 Strategies of War
  b. 28-hour day
  c. 1990 Clean Air Act
  d. Free trade area

23. The _____ is a trilateral trade bloc in North America created by the governments of the United States, Canada, and Mexico. The agreement creating the trade bloc came into force on January 1, 1994. It superseded the Canada-United States Free Trade Agreement between the U.S. and Canada.
  a. Business war game
  b. Trade union
  c. Career portfolios
  d. North American Free Trade Agreement

24. The _____ is an international organization designed by its founders to supervise and liberalize international trade. The organization officially commenced on 1 January 1995, under the Marrakesh Agreement, succeeding the 1947 General Agreement on Tariffs and Trade (GATT.)

The _____ deals with regulation of trade between participating countries; it provides a framework for negotiating and formalising trade agreements, and a dispute resolution process aimed at enforcing participants' adherence to _____ agreements which are signed by representatives of member governments and ratified by their parliaments.

Chapter 2. The Global Environment: Culture, Ethics, and Social Responsibility 21

a. Network planning and design
b. 1990 Clean Air Act
c. National Institute for Occupational Safety and Health
d. World Trade Organization

25. A _____ or transnational corporation is a corporation or enterprise that manages production or delivers services in more than one country. It can also be referred to as an international corporation.

The first modern _____ is generally thought to be the Dutch East India Company, established in 1602.

a. Multinational corporation
b. Financial Accounting Standards Board
c. Command center
d. Small and medium enterprises

26. _____ is exchange of capital, goods, and services across international borders or territories. In most countries, it represents a significant share of gross domestic product (GDP.) While _____ has been present throughout much of history, its economic, social, and political importance has been on the rise in recent centuries.
a. International trade
b. AAAI
c. A Stake in the Outcome
d. A4e

27. _____ is a term used to describe practice of sourcing from the global market for goods and services across geopolitical boundaries. _____ often aims to exploit global efficiencies in the delivery of a product or service. These efficiencies include low cost skilled labor, low cost raw material and other economic factors like tax breaks and low trade tariffs.
a. 1990 Clean Air Act
b. Global sourcing
c. Purchase requisition
d. Purchasing process

28. A _____ or maquila is a factory that imports materials and equipment on a duty-free and tariff-free basis for assembly or manufacturing and then re-exports the assembled product, usually back to the originating country. A maquila is also referred to as a 'twin plant', or 'in-bond' industry. Nearly half a million Mexicans are employed in _____s.

22   Chapter 2. The Global Environment: Culture, Ethics, and Social Responsibility

  a. 28-hour day
  b. 1990 Clean Air Act
  c. 33 Strategies of War
  d. Maquiladora

29. _____ is subcontracting a process, such as product design or manufacturing, to a third-party company. The decision to outsource is often made in the interest of lowering cost or making better use of time and energy costs, redirecting or conserving energy directed at the competencies of a particular business, or to make more efficient use of land, labor, capital, (information) technology and resources. _____ became part of the business lexicon during the 1980s.
  a. Unemployment insurance
  b. Outsourcing
  c. Opinion leadership
  d. Operant conditioning

30. In business, the term word _____ refers to a number of procurement practices, aimed at finding, evaluating and engaging suppliers of goods and services:

- Global _____, a procurement strategy aimed at exploiting global efficiencies in production
- Strategic _____, a component of supply chain management, for improving and re-evaluating purchasing activities
- _____, the identification of job candidates through proactive recruiting technique
- Co-_____, a type of auditing service
- Low-cost country _____, a procurement strategy for acquiring materials from countries with lower labour and production costs in order to cut operating expenses
- Corporate _____, a supply chain, purchasing/procurement, and inventory function
- Second-tier _____, a practice of rewarding suppliers for attempting to achieve minority-owned business spending goals of their customer
- Netsourcing, a practice of utilizing an established group of businesses, individuals, or hardware ' software applications to streamline or initiate procurement practices by tapping in to and working through a third party provider
- Inverted _____, a price volatility reduction strategy usually conducted by procurement or supply-chain person by which the value of an organization's waste-stream is maximized by actively seeking out the highest price possible from a range of potential buyers exploiting price trends and other market factors
- Multisourcing, a strategy that treats a given function, such as IT, as a portfolio of activities, some of which should be outsourced and others of which should be performed by internal staff.
- Crowdsourcing, using an undefined, generally large group of people or community in the form of an open call to perform a task

In journalism, it can also refer to:

- Journalism _____, the practice of identifying a person or publication that gives information
- Single _____, the reuse of content in publishing

In computing, it can refer to:

- Open-_____, the act of releasing previously proprietary software under an open source/free software license
- Power _____ equipment, network devices that will provide power in a Power over Ethernet (PoE) setup

a. Sourcing
b. Cost Management
c. Reinforcement
d. Continuous

31. A _____ is an entity formed between two or more parties to undertake economic activity together. The parties agree to create a new entity by both contributing equity, and they then share in the revenues, expenses, and control of the enterprise. The venture can be for one specific project only, or a continuing business relationship such as the Fuji Xerox _____.
   a. Joint venture
   b. Meritor Savings Bank v. Vinson
   c. Civil Rights Act of 1991
   d. Patent

32. An _____ is a person who has possession of an enterprise and assumes significant accountability for the inherent risks and the outcome. It is an ambitious leader who combines land, labor, and capital to create and market new goods or services. The term is a loanword from French and was first defined by the Irish economist Richard Cantillon.
   a. AAAI
   b. A4e
   c. A Stake in the Outcome
   d. Entrepreneur

33. _____ as defined in business terms is an organization's strategic guide to globalization. A sound _____ should address these questions: what must be (versus what is) the extent of market presence in the world's major markets? How to build the necessary global presence? What must be (versus what is) the optimal locations around the world for the various value chain activities? How to run global presence into global competitive advantage?

Academic research on _____ came of age during the 1980s, including work by Michael Porter and Christopher Bartlett ' Sumantra Ghoshal. Among the forces perceived to bring about the globalization of competition were convergence in economic systems and technological change, especially in information technology, that facilitated and required the coordination of a multinational firm's strategy on a worldwide scale.

a. 1990 Clean Air Act
b. 33 Strategies of War
c. 28-hour day
d. Global strategy

34. _____ has been described as the 'process of social influence in which one person can enlist the aid and support of others in the accomplishment of a common task'. A definition more inclusive of followers comes from Alan Keith of Genentech who said '_____ is ultimately about creating a way for people to contribute to making something extraordinary happen.'

_____ is one of the most salient aspects of the organizational context. However, defining _____ has been challenging.

a. Leadership
b. 1990 Clean Air Act
c. Situational leadership
d. 28-hour day

35. The phrase _____, according to the Organization for Economic Co-operation and Development, refers to 'creative work undertaken on a systematic basis in order to increase the stock of knowledge, including knowledge of man, culture and society, and the use of this stock of knowledge to devise new applications [sic]'

New product design and development is more than often a crucial factor in the survival of a company. In an industry that is fast changing, firms must continually revise their design and range of products. This is necessary due to continuous technology change and development as well as other competitors and the changing preference of customers.

a. Research and development
b. 28-hour day
c. 33 Strategies of War
d. 1990 Clean Air Act

36. _____ is an integrated communications-based process through which individuals and communities discover that existing and newly-identified needs and wants may be satisfied by the products and services of others.

_____ is defined by the American _____ Association as the activity, set of institutions, and processes for creating, communicating, delivering, and exchanging offerings that have value for customers, clients, partners, and society at large. The term developed from the original meaning which referred literally to going to market, as in shopping, or going to a market to buy or sell goods or services.

Chapter 2. The Global Environment: Culture, Ethics, and Social Responsibility 25

a. Market development
b. Disruptive technology
c. Marketing
d. Customer relationship management

37. The 'business case for _____', theorizes that in a global marketplace, a company that employs a diverse workforce (both men and women, people of many generations, people from ethnically and racially diverse backgrounds etc.) is better able to understand the demographics of the marketplace it serves and is thus better equipped to thrive in that marketplace than a company that has a more limited range of employee demographics.

An additional corollary suggests that a company that supports the _____ of its workforce can also improve employee satisfaction, productivity and retention.

a. Diversity
b. Trademark
c. Virtual team
d. Kanban

38. _____, commonly referred to as 'eBusiness' or 'e-Business', may be defined as the utilization of information and communication technologies (ICT) in support of all the activities of business. Commerce constitutes the exchange of products and services between businesses, groups and individuals and hence can be seen as one of the essential activities of any business. Hence, electronic commerce or eCommerce focuses on the use of ICT to enable the external activities and relationships of the business with individuals, groups and other businesses.
a. A Stake in the Outcome
b. A4e
c. AAAI
d. Electronic business

39. The _____ of 2002 (Pub.L. 107-204, 116 Stat. 745, enacted July 30, 2002), also known as the Public Company Accounting Reform and Investor Protection Act of 2002 and commonly called Sarbanes-Oxley, Sarbox or SOX, is a United States federal law enacted on July 30, 2002, as a reaction to a number of major corporate and accounting scandals including those affecting Enron, Tyco International, Adelphia, Peregrine Systems and WorldCom.
a. Sarbanes-Oxley Act
b. Sarbanes-Oxley Act of 2002
c. Letter of credit
d. Fair Labor Standards Act

Chapter 2. The Global Environment: Culture, Ethics, and Social Responsibility

40. _____ is the process by which a new idea or new product is accepted by the market. The rate of _____ is the speed that the new idea spreads from one consumer to the next. Adoption is similar to _____ except that it deals with the psychological processes an individual goes through, rather than an aggregate market process.
   a. Category management
   b. Value chain
   c. Mass marketing
   d. Diffusion

41. _____ is a social phenomenon which tends to occur in groups of people above a certain critical size when responsibility is not explicitly assigned. This phenomenon rarely ever occurs in small groups. In tests, groups of three or fewer, everyone in the group took action as opposed to groups of over ten where in almost every test, no one took action.
   a. Psychometrics
   b. Groupthink
   c. Psychological statistics
   d. Diffusion of responsibility

42. A _____ is an alliance among individuals or groups, during which they cooperate in joint action, each in his own self-interest, joining forces together for a common cause. This alliance may be temporary or a matter of convenience. A _____ thus differs from a more formal covenant.
   a. 1990 Clean Air Act
   b. 33 Strategies of War
   c. Coalition
   d. 28-hour day

43. The general definition of an _____ is an evaluation of a person, organization, system, process, project or product. _____s are performed to ascertain the validity and reliability of information; also to provide an assessment of a system's internal control. The goal of an _____ is to express an opinion on the person / organization/system (etc) in question, under evaluation based on work done on a test basis.
   a. Internal control
   b. Audit committee
   c. A Stake in the Outcome
   d. Audit

44. A _____ is one of several ways of doing research whether it is social science related or even socially related. It is an intensive study of a single group, incident, or community. Other ways include experiments, surveys, multiple histories, and analysis of archival information .

Rather than using samples and following a rigid protocol to examine limited number of variables, _____ methods involve an in-depth, longitudinal examination of a single instance or event: a case.

a. Longitudinal study
b. Case study
c. Standard operating procedure
d. 1990 Clean Air Act

Chapter 3. Creative Problem Solving and Decision Making

1. _____ can be regarded as an outcome of mental processes (cognitive process) leading to the selection of a course of action among several alternatives. Every _____ process produces a final choice. The output can be an action or an opinion of choice.
   a. 1990 Clean Air Act
   b. 33 Strategies of War
   c. 28-hour day
   d. Decision making

2. The _____ (Situation, Task, Action, Result) format is a job interview technique used by interviewers to gather all the relevant information about a specific capability that the job requires. This interview format is said to have a higher degree of predictability of future on-the-job performance than the traditional interview.

   - Situation: The interviewer wants you to present a recent challenge and situation in which you found yourself.
   - Task: What did you have to achieve? The interviewer will be looking to see what you were trying to achieve from the situation.
   - Action: What did you do? The interviewer will be looking for information on what you did, why you did it and what were the alternatives.
   - Results: What was the outcome of your actions? What did you achieve through your actions and did you meet your objectives. What did you learn from this experience and have you used this learning since?

   a. Phrase completion
   b. Star
   c. Competency-based job descriptions
   d. Rasch models

3. _____ is a range of processes aimed at alleviating or eliminating sources of conflict. The term '_____' is sometimes used interchangeably with the term dispute resolution or alternative dispute resolution. Processes of _____ generally include negotiation, mediation and diplomacy.
   a. 33 Strategies of War
   b. 28-hour day
   c. 1990 Clean Air Act
   d. Conflict resolution

4. A _____ is a list of the general tasks and responsibilities of a position. Typically, it also includes to whom the position reports, specifications such as the qualifications needed by the person in the job, salary range for the position, etc. A _____ is usually developed by conducting a job analysis, which includes examining the tasks and sequences of tasks necessary to perform the job.

a. Job description
b. Recruitment
c. Recruitment Process Insourcing
d. Recruitment advertising

5. _____ of the learning curve effect and the closely related experience curve effect express the relationship between equations for experience and efficiency or between efficiency gains and investment in the effort. The experience of 'learning curves' was first observed by the 19th Century German psychologist Hermann Ebbinghaus according to the difficulty of memorizing varying numbers of verbal stimuli, and subsequent learning about the complex processes of learning are discussed in the

The rule used for representing the learning curve effect states that the more times a task has been performed, the less time will be required on each subsequent iteration.

a. Spatial Decision Support Systems
b. Distribution
c. Models
d. Point biserial correlation coefficient

6. In decision theory and estimation theory, the _____ of an estimator, $\hat{\theta}$, of an unknown parameter of the distribution, θ, is the expected value of the loss function

$$R(\theta, \hat{\theta}) = \mathbb{E}_\theta L(\theta, \hat{\theta}) = \int L(\theta, \hat{\theta}) \, dP_\theta.$$

where dP_θ is a probability measure parametrized by θ.

- For a scalar parameter θ and a quadratic loss function,

$$L(\theta, \hat{\theta}) = (\theta - \hat{\theta})^2$$

the _____ function becomes the mean squared error of the estimate,

$$R(\theta, \hat{\theta}) = E_\theta(\theta - \hat{\theta})^2$$

- In density estimation, the unknown parameter is probability density itself. The loss function is typically chosen to be a norm in an appropriate function space. For example, for L^2 norm,

$$L(f, \hat{f}) = \|f - \hat{f}\|_2^2$$

the _____ function becomes the mean integrated squared error

$$R(f, \hat{f}) = E\|f - \hat{f}\|^2$$

a. Risk aversion
b. Financial modeling
c. Risk
d. Linear model

7. _____ is a concept based on the fact that rationality of individuals is limited by the information they have, the cognitive limitations of their minds, and the finite amount of time they have to make decisions. This contrasts with the concept of rationality as optimization. Another way to look at _____ is that, because decision-makers lack the ability and resources to arrive at the optimal solution, they instead apply their rationality only after having greatly simplified the choices available.
a. Complete information
b. Mixed strategy
c. Transferable utility
d. Bounded rationality

8. _____ is decision making in groups consisting of multiple members/entities. The challenge of group decision is deciding what action a group should take. There are various systems designed to solve this problem.

a. Collaborative Planning, Forecasting and Replenishment
b. Genbutsu
c. Control of Substances Hazardous to Health Regulations 2002
d. Groups decision making

9. _____ is a type of thought exhibited by group members who try to minimize conflict and reach consensus without critically testing, analyzing, and evaluating ideas. Individual creativity, uniqueness, and independent thinking are lost in the pursuit of group cohesiveness, as are the advantages of reasonable balance in choice and thought that might normally be obtained by making decisions as a group. During _____, members of the group avoid promoting viewpoints outside the comfort zone of consensus thinking.
   a. Diffusion of responsibility
   b. Groupthink
   c. Psychological statistics
   d. Self-report inventory

10. _____ is a concept in ethics with several meanings. It is often used synonymously with such concepts as responsibility, answerability, enforcement, blameworthiness, liability and other terms associated with the expectation of account-giving. As an aspect of governance, it has been central to discussions related to problems in both the public and private (corporation) worlds.
    a. Usury
    b. A4e
    c. A Stake in the Outcome
    d. Accountability

11. The process of _____ involves the introduction of a good or service that is new or substantially improved. This includes, but is not limited to, improvements in functional characteristics, technical abilities, or ease of use.
    a. Service-profit chain
    b. Product innovation
    c. Job enlargement
    d. Letter of resignation

12. _____ is a group creativity technique designed to generate a large number of ideas for the solution of a problem. The method was first popularized in the late 1930s by Alex Faickney Osborn in a book called Applied Imagination. Osborn proposed that groups could double their creative output with _____.

a. Abraham Harold Maslow
b. Adam Smith
c. Affiliation
d. Brainstorming

13. The _____ is a systematic, interactive forecasting method which relies on a panel of independent experts. The carefully selected experts answer questionnaires in two or more rounds. After each round, a facilitator provides an anonymous summary of the experts' forecasts from the previous round as well as the reasons they provided for their judgments.

a. Learning organization
b. Quality function deployment
c. Hoshin Kanri
d. Delphi method

14. A _____ is a decision support tool that uses a tree-like graph or model of decisions and their possible consequences, including chance event outcomes, resource costs, and utility. _____s are commonly used in operations research, specifically in decision analysis, to help identify a strategy most likely to reach a goal. Another use of _____s is as a descriptive means for calculating conditional probabilities.

a. 1990 Clean Air Act
b. 33 Strategies of War
c. Decision tree
d. 28-hour day

15. _____ is the planning process used to determine whether a firm's long term investments such as new machinery, replacement machinery, new plants, new products, and research development projects are worth pursuing. It is budget for major capital, or investment, expenditures.

Many formal methods are used in _____, including the techniques such as

- Net present value
- Profitability index
- Internal rate of return
- Modified Internal Rate of Return
- Equivalent annuity

These methods use the incremental cash flows from each potential investment, or project. Techniques based on accounting earnings and accounting rules are sometimes used - though economists consider this to be improper - such as the accounting rate of return, and 'return on investment.' Simplified and hybrid methods are used as well, such as payback period and discounted payback period.

a. Restricted stock
b. Gross profit
c. Gross profit margin
d. Capital budgeting

16. In finance, the _____ approach describes a method of valuing a project, company, or asset using the concepts of the time value of money. All future cash flows are estimated and discounted to give their present values. The discount rate used is generally the appropriate WACC, that reflects the risk of the cashflows.

a. Net present value
b. 1990 Clean Air Act
c. Discounted cash flow
d. Present value

17. In mathematics, _____ is a technique for optimization of a linear objective function, subject to linear equality and linear inequality constraints. Informally, _____ determines the way to achieve the best outcome (such as maximum profit or lowest cost) in a given mathematical model and given some list of requirements represented as linear equations.

More formally, given a polytope (for example, a polygon or a polyhedron), and a real-valued affine function

$$f(x_1, x_2, \ldots, x_n) = c_1 x_1 + c_2 x_2 + \cdots + c_n x_n + d$$

defined on this polytope, a _____ method will find a point in the polytope where this function has the smallest (or largest) value.

a. 1990 Clean Air Act
b. Slack variable
c. Linear programming
d. Linear programming relaxation

18. Procter is a surname, and may also refer to:

- Bryan Waller Procter (pseud. Barry Cornwall), English poet
- Goodwin Procter, American law firm
- _____, consumer products multinational

a. Master and Servant Acts
b. Downstream
c. Strict liability
d. Procter ' Gamble

19. _____ refers to the movement of cash into or out of a business or financial product. It is usually measured during a specified, finite period of time. Measurement of _____ can be used

- to determine a project's rate of return or value. The time of _____s into and out of projects are used as inputs in financial models such as internal rate of return, and net present value.
- to determine problems with a business's liquidity. Being profitable does not necessarily mean being liquid. A company can fail because of a shortage of cash, even while profitable.
- as an alternate measure of a business's profits when it is believed that accrual accounting concepts do not represent economic realities. For example, a company may be notionally profitable but generating little operational cash (as may be the case for a company that barters its products rather than selling for cash.) In such a case, the company may be deriving additional operating cash by issuing shares evaluating default risk, re-investment requirements, etc.

_____ is a generic term used differently depending on the context. It may be defined by users for their own purposes.

a. Sweat equity
b. Gross profit margin
c. Cash flow
d. Gross profit

20. _____ is a way of expressing knowledge or belief that an event will occur or has occurred. In mathematics the concept has been given an exact meaning in _____ theory, that is used extensively in such areas of study as mathematics, statistics, finance, gambling, science, and philosophy to draw conclusions about the likelihood of potential events and the underlying mechanics of complex systems.

The word _____ does not have a consistent direct definition.

a. Probability
b. Time series analysis
c. Standard deviation
d. Statistics

21. _____ is the branch of mathematics concerned with analysis of random phenomena. The central objects of _____ are random variables, stochastic processes, and events: mathematical abstractions of non-deterministic events or measured quantities that may either be single occurrences or evolve over time in an apparently random fashion. Although an individual coin toss or the roll of a die is a random event, if repeated many times the sequence of random events will exhibit certain statistical patterns, which can be studied and predicted.
   a. Probability vector
   b. Probability mass function
   c. Fuzzy measure theory
   d. Probability theory

22.

Founded in 1958 by Dr. Charles Kepner and Dr. Benjamin Tregoe, _____, Inc., is a global organisation providing consulting and training services around problem solving, decision making and project execution methodologies.

_____'s trademark technique, Rational Process, which is commonly referred to as the 'KT Process', is the creation of structured, systematic processes which are used to maximise the critical thinking skills of key stakeholders in a particular situation, problem (potential or real), decision or opportunity.

The Rational Processes are broken down into the following:SITUATION APPRAISAL - the process of ensuring that priority and order are established for multiple concerns associated with a specific issue.Example - The company's in-house built payroll system is becoming outdated and increasingly difficult to support.

   a. Hierarchical Decision Process
   b. Multi-Criteria Decision Analysis
   c. Multi-Attribute Global Inference of Quality
   d. Kepner-Tregoe

23. _____ is a term that refers both to:

- a formal discipline used to help appraise, or assess, the case for a project or proposal, which itself is a process known as project appraisal; and
- an informal approach to making decisions of any kind.

Under both definitions the process involves, whether explicitly or implicitly, weighing the total expected costs against the total expected benefits of one or more actions in order to choose the best or most profitable option. The formal process is often referred to as either CBA (_____) or BCost-benefit analysis

A hallmark of CBA is that all benefits and all costs are expressed in money terms, and are adjusted for the time value of money, so that all flows of benefits and flows of project costs over time (which tend to occur at different points in time) are expressed on a common basis in terms of their 'present value.' Closely related, but slightly different, formal techniques include Cost-effectiveness analysis, Economic impact analysis, Fiscal impact analysis and Social Return on Investment(SROI) analysis. The latter builds upon the logic of _____, but differs in that it is explicitly designed to inform the practical decision-making of enterprise managers and investors focused on optimising their social and environmental impacts.

   a. Decision engineering
   b. Cost-benefit analysis
   c. Kepner-Tregoe
   d. Gittins index

24. _____-model (SCOR(r)) is a process reference model developed by the management consulting firm PRTM and AMR Research and endorsed by the Supply-Chain Council (SCC) as the cross-industry de facto standard diagnostic tool for supply chain management. SCOR enables users to address, improve, and communicate supply chain management practices within and between all interested parties in the Extended Enterprise.

SCOR(r) is a management tool, spanning from the supplier's supplier to the customer's customer. The model has been developed by the members of the Council on a volunteer basis to describe the business activities associated with all phases of satisfying a customer's demand.

   a. Delayed differentiation
   b. Supply Chain Risk Management
   c. Supply-Chain Operations Reference
   d. Supply chain management software

25. A _____ is a working environment with conditions that are considered by many people of industrialized nations to be difficult or dangerous, usually where the workers have few opportunities to address their situation. This can include exposure to harmful materials, hazardous situations, extreme temperatures, or abuse from employers. _____ workers often work long hours for little pay, regardless of any laws mandating overtime pay or a minimum wage.
   a. Continuous
   b. Complement
   c. Rate of return
   d. Sweatshop

26. _____ , also referred to simply as a 'public offering' or 'flotation,' is when a company issues common stock or shares to the public for the first time. They are often issued by smaller, younger companies seeking capital to expand, but can also be done by large privately-owned companies looking to become publicly traded.

Chapter 3. Creative Problem Solving and Decision Making

In an _____ the issuer may obtain the assistance of an underwriting firm, which helps it determine what type of security to issue (common or preferred), best offering price and time to bring it to market.

a. Occupational Safety and Health Administration
b. Outsourcing
c. Unemployment insurance
d. Initial public offering

27. _____ is an advertisement in which a particular product specifically mentions a competitor by name for the express purpose of showing why the competitor is inferior to the product naming it.

This should not be confused with parody advertisements, where a fictional product is being advertised for the purpose of poking fun at the particular advertisement, nor should it be confused with the use of a coined brand name for the purpose of comparing the product without actually naming an actual competitor. ('Wikipedia tastes better and is less filling than the Encyclopedia Galactica.')

In the 1980s, during what has been referred to as the cola wars, soft-drink manufacturer Pepsi ran a series of advertisements where people, caught on hidden camera, in a blind taste test, chose Pepsi over rival Coca-Cola.

a. Comparative advertising
b. 28-hour day
c. 33 Strategies of War
d. 1990 Clean Air Act

28. _____ is one of the managerial functions like planning, organizing, staffing and directing. It is an important function because it helps to check the errors and to take the corrective action so that deviation from standards are minimized and stated goals of the organization are achieved in desired manner. According to modern concepts, _____ is a foreseeing action whereas earlier concept of _____ was used only when errors were detected. _____ in management means setting standards, measuring actual performance and taking corrective action.

a. Turnover
b. Control
c. Decision tree pruning
d. Schedule of reinforcement

29. The phrase mergers and _____s refers to the aspect of corporate strategy, corporate finance and management dealing with the buying, selling and combining of different companies that can aid, finance, or help a growing company in a given industry grow rapidly without having to create another business entity.

An _____, also known as a takeover or a buyout, is the buying of one company (the 'target') by another. An _____ may be friendly or hostile.

a. Acquisition
b. AAAI
c. A4e
d. A Stake in the Outcome

30. A _____ is one of several ways of doing research whether it is social science related or even socially related. It is an intensive study of a single group, incident, or community. Other ways include experiments, surveys, multiple histories, and analysis of archival information .

Rather than using samples and following a rigid protocol to examine limited number of variables, _____ methods involve an in-depth, longitudinal examination of a single instance or event: a case.

a. 1990 Clean Air Act
b. Longitudinal study
c. Standard operating procedure
d. Case study

Chapter 4. Strategic and Operational Planning   39

1. An _____ is a subset of strategic work plan. It describes short-term ways of achieving milestones and explains how, or what portion of, a strategic plan will be put into operation during a given operational period, in the case of commercial application, a fiscal year or another given budgetary term. An operational plan is the basis for, and justification of an annual operating budget request.
   a. A Stake in the Outcome
   b. A4e
   c. Operational planning
   d. AAAI

2. _____ is an organization's process of defining its strategy and making decisions on allocating its resources to pursue this strategy, including its capital and people. Various business analysis techniques can be used in _____, including SWOT analysis (Strengths, Weaknesses, Opportunities, and Threats) and PEST analysis (Political, Economic, Social, and Technological analysis) or STEER analysis involving Socio-cultural, Technological, Economic, Ecological, and Regulatory factors and EPISTEL (Environment, Political, Informatic, Social, Technological, Economic and Legal)

_____ is the formal consideration of an organization's future course. All _____ deals with at least one of three key questions:

   1. 'What do we do?'
   2. 'For whom do we do it?'
   3. 'How do we excel?'

In business _____, the third question is better phrased 'How can we beat or avoid competition?'. (Bradford and Duncan, page 1.)

   a. 33 Strategies of War
   b. 28-hour day
   c. 1990 Clean Air Act
   d. Strategic planning

3. _____ is a business Advocate term for an element which is necessary for an organization or project to achieve its mission. They are the critical factors or activities required for ensuring the success of your business. The term was initially used in the world of data analysis, and business analysis.
   a. Customer satisfaction
   b. Business hours
   c. Collaborative leadership
   d. Critical success factor

4. _____ is a strategic planning method used to evaluate the Strengths, Weaknesses, Opportunities, and Threats involved in a project or in a business venture. It involves specifying the objective of the business venture or project and identifying the internal and external factors that are favorable and unfavorable to achieving that objective. The technique is credited to Albert Humphrey, who led a convention at Stanford University in the 1960s and 1970s using data from Fortune 500 companies.

   a. Marketing
   b. SWOT analysis
   c. Market share
   d. Corporate image

5. _____ is the process of comparing the cost, cycle time, productivity, or quality of a specific process or method to another that is widely considered to be an industry standard or best practice. Essentially, _____ provides a snapshot of the performance of your business and helps you understand where you are in relation to a particular standard. The result is often a business case for making changes in order to make improvements.

   a. Competitive heterogeneity
   b. Cost leadership
   c. Complementors
   d. Benchmarking

6. _____ is something that a firm can do well and that meets the following three conditions:

Competencies are things that companys execute well across several business units or product sectors.

Firms usually have few competencies, but these are usually less liable to change rapidly.

1. It provides consumer benefits
2. It is not easy for competitors to imitate
3. It can be leveraged widely to many products and markets.

A _____ can take various forms, including technical/subject matter know-how, a reliable process and/or close relationships with customers and suppliers (Mascarenhas et al. 1998.)

   a. Dominant Design
   b. Core competency
   c. NAIRU
   d. Learning-by-doing

7. _____ is a process of agreeing upon objectives within an organization so that management and employees agree to the objectives and understand what they are in the organization.

Chapter 4. Strategic and Operational Planning

The term '_____' was first popularized by Peter Drucker in his 1954 book 'The Practice of Management'.

The essence of _____ is participative goal setting, choosing course of actions and decision making.

   a. Management by Objectives
   b. Business economics
   c. Clean sheet review
   d. Job enrichment

8. A _____ is a name or trademark connected with a product or producer. _____s have become increasingly important components of culture and the economy, now being described as 'cultural accessories and personal philosophies'.

Some people distinguish the psychological aspect of a _____ from the experiential aspect.

   a. Brand
   b. Brand awareness
   c. Brand extension
   d. Brand loyalty

9. _____ is understood as a business unit within the overall corporate identity which is distinguishable from other business because it serves a defined external market where management can conduct strategic planning in relation to products and markets. When companies become really large, they are best thought of as being composed of a number of businesses (or _____s.)

In the broader domain of strategic management, the phrase '_____' came into use in the 1960s, largely as a result of General Electric's many units.

   a. Switching cost
   b. Strategic group
   c. Strategic drift
   d. Strategic business unit

10. In business, a _____ is a product or a business unit that generates unusually high profit margins: so high that it is responsible for a large amount of a company's operating profit. This profit far exceeds the amount necessary to maintain the _____ business, and the excess is used by the business for other purposes.

A firm is said to be acting as a _____ when its earnings per share (EPS) is equal to its dividends per share (DPS), or in other words, when a firm pays out 100% of its free cash flow (FCF) to its shareholders as dividends at the end of each accounting term.

a. Design management in organization
b. Cash cow
c. Middle management
d. Workflow

11. In decision theory and estimation theory, the _____ of an estimator, $\hat{\theta}$, of an unknown parameter of the distribution, θ, is the expected value of the loss function

$$R(\theta, \hat{\theta}) = \mathbb{E}_\theta L(\theta, \hat{\theta}) = \int L(\theta, \hat{\theta})\, dP_\theta.$$

where dP_θ is a probability measure parametrized by θ.

- For a scalar parameter θ and a quadratic loss function,

$$L(\theta, \hat{\theta}) = (\theta - \hat{\theta})^2$$

  the _____ function becomes the mean squared error of the estimate,

$$R(\theta, \hat{\theta}) = E_\theta (\theta - \hat{\theta})^2$$

- In density estimation, the unknown parameter is probability density itself. The loss function is typically chosen to be a norm in an appropriate function space. For example, for L^2 norm,

$$L(f, \hat{f}) = \|f - \hat{f}\|_2^2$$

  the _____ function becomes the mean integrated squared error

$$R(f, \hat{f}) = E\|f - \hat{f}\|^2$$

a. Risk
b. Financial modeling
c. Linear model
d. Risk aversion

12. The _____ (Situation, Task, Action, Result) format is a job interview technique used by interviewers to gather all the relevant information about a specific capability that the job requires. This interview format is said to have a higher degree of predictability of future on-the-job performance than the traditional interview.

- Situation: The interviewer wants you to present a recent challenge and situation in which you found yourself.
- Task: What did you have to achieve? The interviewer will be looking to see what you were trying to achieve from the situation.
- Action: What did you do? The interviewer will be looking for information on what you did, why you did it and what were the alternatives.
- Results: What was the outcome of your actions? What did you achieve through your actions and did you meet your objectives. What did you learn from this experience and have you used this learning since?

a. Star
b. Rasch models
c. Phrase completion
d. Competency-based job descriptions

13. Procter is a surname, and may also refer to:

- Bryan Waller Procter (pseud. Barry Cornwall), English poet
- Goodwin Procter, American law firm
- _____, consumer products multinational

a. Downstream
b. Master and Servant Acts
c. Procter ' Gamble
d. Strict liability

14. In economics, business, retail, and accounting, a _____ is the value of money that has been used up to produce something, and hence is not available for use anymore. In economics, a _____ is an alternative that is given up as a result of a decision. In business, the _____ may be one of acquisition, in which case the amount of money expended to acquire it is counted as _____.

a. Cost
b. Cost overrun
c. Cost allocation
d. Fixed costs

15. _____ is a concept developed by Michael Porter, used in business strategy. It describes a way to establish the competitive advantage. _____, in basic words, means the lowest cost of operation in the industry.

a. Strategic business unit
b. Strategic group
c. Switching cost
d. Cost leadership

16. _____ Management is the succession of strategies used by management as a product goes through its _____. The conditions in which a product is sold changes over time and must be managed as it moves through its succession of stages.

The _____ goes through many phases, involves many professional disciplines, and requires many skills, tools and processes.

a. Golden handshake
b. Strategic Alliance
c. Product life cycle
d. Job hunting

17. _____ has been described as the 'process of social influence in which one person can enlist the aid and support of others in the accomplishment of a common task'. A definition more inclusive of followers comes from Alan Keith of Genentech who said '_____ is ultimately about creating a way for people to contribute to making something extraordinary happen.'

_____ is one of the most salient aspects of the organizational context. However, defining _____ has been challenging.

a. 28-hour day
b. Leadership
c. Situational leadership
d. 1990 Clean Air Act

Chapter 4. Strategic and Operational Planning

18. _____ is an increasingly broadening term with which an organization, or other human system describes the combination of traditionally administrative personnel functions with acquisition and application of skills, knowledge and experience, Employee Relations and resource planning at various levels. The field draws upon concepts developed in Industrial/Organizational Psychology and System Theory. _____ has at least two related interpretations depending on context. The original usage derives from political economy and economics, where it was traditionally called labor, one of four factors of production although this perspective is changing as a function of new and ongoing research into more strategic approaches at national levels. This first usage is used more in terms of '_____ development', and can go beyond just organizations to the level of nations . The more traditional usage within corporations and businesses refers to the individuals within a firm or agency, and to the portion of the organization that deals with hiring, firing, training, and other personnel issues, typically referred to as `_____ management'.

   a. Bradford Factor
   b. Progressive discipline
   c. Human resources
   d. Human resource management

19. _____ is an integrated communications-based process through which individuals and communities discover that existing and newly-identified needs and wants may be satisfied by the products and services of others.

   _____ is defined by the American _____ Association as the activity, set of institutions, and processes for creating, communicating, delivering, and exchanging offerings that have value for customers, clients, partners, and society at large. The term developed from the original meaning which referred literally to going to market, as in shopping, or going to a market to buy or sell goods or services.

   a. Market development
   b. Marketing
   c. Customer relationship management
   d. Disruptive technology

20. A _____ is a process that can allow an organization to concentrate its limited resources on the greatest opportunities to increase sales and achieve a sustainable competitive advantage. A _____ should be centered around the key concept that customer satisfaction is the main goal.

   A _____ is a written plan which combines product development, promotion, distribution, and pricing approach, identifies the firm's marketing goals, and explains how they will be achieved within a stated timeframe.

   a. Product bundling
   b. Disruptive technology
   c. Category management
   d. Marketing strategy

Chapter 4. Strategic and Operational Planning

21. The phrase _____, according to the Organization for Economic Co-operation and Development, refers to 'creative work undertaken on a systematic basis in order to increase the stock of knowledge, including knowledge of man, culture and society, and the use of this stock of knowledge to devise new applications [sic]'

New product design and development is more than often a crucial factor in the survival of a company. In an industry that is fast changing, firms must continually revise their design and range of products. This is necessary due to continuous technology change and development as well as other competitors and the changing preference of customers.

   a. Research and development
   b. 28-hour day
   c. 33 Strategies of War
   d. 1990 Clean Air Act

22. A _____ is a set of instructions having the force of a directive, covering those features of operations that lend themselves to a definite or standardized procedure without loss of effectiveness. Standard Operating Policies and Procedures can be effective catalysts to drive performance improvement and improving organizational results.
   a. 1990 Clean Air Act
   b. Standard operating procedure
   c. Longitudinal study
   d. Risk-benefit analysis

23. A _____ is a plan devised for a specific situation when things could go wrong. _____s are often devised by governments or businesses who want to be prepared for anything that could happen. They are sometimes known as 'Back-up plans', 'Worst-case scenario plans' or 'Plan B'.
   a. Contingency plan
   b. 1990 Clean Air Act
   c. 33 Strategies of War
   d. 28-hour day

24. A _____ is one of several ways of doing research whether it is social science related or even socially related. It is an intensive study of a single group, incident, or community.Other ways include experiments, surveys, multiple histories, and analysis of archival information .

Rather than using samples and following a rigid protocol to examine limited number of variables, _____ methods involve an in-depth, longitudinal examination of a single instance or event: a case.

a. Standard operating procedure
b. 1990 Clean Air Act
c. Longitudinal study
d. Case study

25. _____ refers to a range of skills, tools, and techniques used to manage time when accomplishing specific tasks, projects and goals. This set encompass a wide scope of activities, and these include planning, allocating, setting goals, delegation, analysis of time spent, monitoring, organizing, scheduling, and prioritizing. Initially _____ referred to just business or work activities, but eventually the term broadened to include personal activities also.
   a. Formula for Change
   b. Voice of the customer
   c. Cash cow
   d. Time Management

Chapter 5. Organizing and Delegating Work

1. A _____ is a process in which a potential employee is evaluated by an employer for prospective employment in their company, organization and was established in the late 16th century.

A _____ typically precedes the hiring decision, and is used to evaluate the candidate. The interview is usually preceded by the evaluation of submitted résumés from interested candidates, then selecting a small number of candidates for interviews.

 a. Job interview
 b. Split shift
 c. Supported employment
 d. Payrolling

2. In a military context, the _____ is the line of authority and responsibility along which orders are passed within a military unit and between different units. The term is also used in a civilian management context describing comparable hierarchical structures of authority.
 a. 1990 Clean Air Act
 b. 28-hour day
 c. French leave
 d. Chain of command

3. The _____ is a standardized, on-scene, all-hazard incident management concept. It is a management protocol originally designed for emergency management agencies in the United States which was later federalized there. It has since been adopted by agencies in other countries.
 a. Incident Command Structure
 b. A Stake in the Outcome
 c. AAAI
 d. A4e

4. _____ is an organization's process of defining its strategy and making decisions on allocating its resources to pursue this strategy, including its capital and people. Various business analysis techniques can be used in _____, including SWOT analysis (Strengths, Weaknesses, Opportunities, and Threats) and PEST analysis (Political, Economic, Social, and Technological analysis) or STEER analysis involving Socio-cultural, Technological, Economic, Ecological, and Regulatory factors and EPISTEL (Environment, Political, Informatic, Social, Technological, Economic and Legal)

_____ is the formal consideration of an organization's future course. All _____ deals with at least one of three key questions:

 1. 'What do we do?'
 2. 'For whom do we do it?'
 3. 'How do we excel?'

Chapter 5. Organizing and Delegating Work   49

In business _____, the third question is better phrased 'How can we beat or avoid competition?'. (Bradford and Duncan, page 1.)

a. 1990 Clean Air Act
b. Strategic planning
c. 28-hour day
d. 33 Strategies of War

5. _____(known as horizontal organization) refers to an organizational structure with few or no levels of intervening management between staff and managers. The idea is that well-trained workers will be more productive when they are more directly involved in the decision making process, rather than closely supervised by many layers of management.

This structure is generally possible only in smaller organizations or individual units within larger organizations.

a. 1990 Clean Air Act
b. 33 Strategies of War
c. 28-hour day
d. Flat organization

6. _____ is a concept in ethics with several meanings. It is often used synonymously with such concepts as responsibility, answerability, enforcement, blameworthiness, liability and other terms associated with the expectation of account-giving. As an aspect of governance, it has been central to discussions related to problems in both the public and private (corporation) worlds.
   a. Usury
   b. A4e
   c. Accountability
   d. A Stake in the Outcome

7. An _____, or organogram(me)) is a diagram that shows the structure of an organization and the relationships and relative ranks of its parts and positions/jobs. The term is also used for similar diagrams, for example ones showing the different elements of a field of knowledge or a group of languages. The French Encyclopédie had one of the first _____s of knowledge in general.
   a. AAAI
   b. A4e
   c. A Stake in the Outcome
   d. Organizational chart

8. _____ refers to the process of grouping activities into departments.

Division of labour creates specialists who need coordination. This coordination is facilitated by grouping specialists together in departments.

   a. Maximum wage
   b. Division of labour
   c. Decent work
   d. Departmentalization

9. Procter is a surname, and may also refer to:

- Bryan Waller Procter (pseud. Barry Cornwall), English poet
- Goodwin Procter, American law firm
- _____, consumer products multinational

   a. Downstream
   b. Strict liability
   c. Procter ' Gamble
   d. Master and Servant Acts

10. A _____ is the term given to a company that facilitates the learning of its members and continuously transforms itself. _____s develop as a result of the pressures facing modern organizations and enables them to remain competitive in the business environment. A _____ has five main features; systems thinking, personal mastery, mental models, shared vision and team learning.
   a. Quality function deployment
   b. Hoshin Kanri
   c. 1990 Clean Air Act
   d. Learning organization

11. In mathematical logic, _____ is a valid argument and rule of inference which makes the inference that, if the conjunction A and B is true, then A is true, and B is true.

In formal language:

$$A \wedge B \vdash A$$

Chapter 5. Organizing and Delegating Work

or

$$A \wedge B \vdash B$$

The argument has one premise, namely a conjunction, and one often uses _____ in longer arguments to derive one of the conjuncts.

An example in English:

It's raining and it's pouring.

a. 1990 Clean Air Act
b. Validity
c. Fuzzy logic
d. Simplification

12. _____ refers to training in different ways to improve overall performance. It takes advantage of the particular effectiveness of each training method, while at the same time attempting to neglect the shortcomings of that method by combining it with other methods that address its weaknesses.

Cross training is employee-employer field means, training employees to do one another's work.

a. 28-hour day
b. 1990 Clean Air Act
c. 33 Strategies of War
d. Cross-training

13. _____ describes the situation when output from (or information about the result of) an event or phenomenon in the past will influence the same event/phenomenon in the present or future. When an event is part of a chain of cause-and-effect that forms a circuit or loop, then the event is said to 'feed back' into itself.

_____ is also a synonym for:

- _____ signal; the information about the initial event that is the basis for subsequent modification of the event.
- _____ loop; the causal path that leads from the initial generation of the _____ signal to the subsequent modification of the event.

_____ is a mechanism, process or signal that is looped back to control a system within itself. Such a loop is called a _____ loop.

a. 1990 Clean Air Act
b. Feedback loop
c. Positive feedback
d. Feedback

14. A _____ is one of several ways of doing research whether it is social science related or even socially related. It is an intensive study of a single group, incident, or community. Other ways include experiments, surveys, multiple histories, and analysis of archival information .

Rather than using samples and following a rigid protocol to examine limited number of variables, _____ methods involve an in-depth, longitudinal examination of a single instance or event: a case.

a. 1990 Clean Air Act
b. Longitudinal study
c. Standard operating procedure
d. Case study

Chapter 6. Managing Change: Innovation and Diversity

1. The _____ captures an expanded spectrum of values and criteria for measuring organizational success: economic, ecological and social. With the ratification of the United Nations and ICLEI _____ standard for urban and community accounting in early 2007, this became the dominant approach to public sector full cost accounting. Similar UN standards apply to natural capital and human capital measurement to assist in measurements required by _____, e.g. the ecoBudget standard for reporting ecological footprint.
   a. 1990 Clean Air Act
   b. 33 Strategies of War
   c. 28-hour day
   d. Triple bottom line

2. A _____ is a list of the general tasks and responsibilities of a position. Typically, it also includes to whom the position reports, specifications such as the qualifications needed by the person in the job, salary range for the position, etc. A _____ is usually developed by conducting a job analysis, which includes examining the tasks and sequences of tasks necessary to perform the job.
   a. Recruitment advertising
   b. Recruitment Process Insourcing
   c. Recruitment
   d. Job description

3. _____ is the use of control systems (such as numerical control, programmable logic control, and other industrial control systems), in concert with other applications of information technology (such as computer-aided technologies [CAD, CAM, CAx]), to control industrial machinery and processes, reducing the need for human intervention. In the scope of industrialization, _____ is a step beyond mechanization. Whereas mechanization provided human operators with machinery to assist them with the physical requirements of work, _____ greatly reduces the need for human sensory and mental requirements as well.
   a. A4e
   b. AAAI
   c. Automation
   d. A Stake in the Outcome

4. _____ refers to training in different ways to improve overall performance. It takes advantage of the particular effectiveness of each training method, while at the same time attempting to neglect the shortcomings of that method by combining it with other methods that address its weaknesses.

Cross training is employee-employer field means, training employees to do one another's work.

Chapter 6. Managing Change: Innovation and Diversity

   a. 33 Strategies of War
   b. 1990 Clean Air Act
   c. 28-hour day
   d. Cross-training

5. _____ is a structured approach to transitioning individuals, teams, and organizations from a current state to a desired future state. The current definition of _____ includes both organizational _____ processes and individual _____ models, which together are used to manage the people side of change.

A number of models are available for understanding the transitioning of individuals through the phases of _____ and strengthening organizational development initiative in both government and corporate sectors.

   a. 1990 Clean Air Act
   b. Change management
   c. 33 Strategies of War
   d. 28-hour day

6. _____ is one of the managerial functions like planning, organizing, staffing and directing. It is an important function because it helps to check the errors and to take the corrective action so that deviation from standards are minimized and stated goals of the organization are achieved in desired manner. According to modern concepts, _____ is a foreseeing action whereas earlier concept of _____ was used only when errors were detected. _____ in management means setting standards, measuring actual performance and taking corrective action.
   a. Control
   b. Schedule of reinforcement
   c. Turnover
   d. Decision tree pruning

7. The process of _____ involves the introduction of a good or service that is new or substantially improved. This includes, but is not limited to, improvements in functional characteristics, technical abilities, or ease of use.
   a. Product innovation
   b. Job enlargement
   c. Service-profit chain
   d. Letter of resignation

8. _____ is the practice of using entrepreneurial skills without taking on the risks or accountability associated with entrepreneurial activities. It is practiced by employees within an established organization using a business model. Employees, perhaps engaged in a special project within a larger firm are supposed to behave as entrepreneurs, even though they have the resources and capabilities of the larger firm to draw upon.

Chapter 6. Managing Change: Innovation and Diversity 55

a. Intrapreneurship
b. AAAI
c. A4e
d. A Stake in the Outcome

9. Procter is a surname, and may also refer to:

- Bryan Waller Procter (pseud. Barry Cornwall), English poet
- Goodwin Procter, American law firm
- _____, consumer products multinational

a. Downstream
b. Master and Servant Acts
c. Strict liability
d. Procter ' Gamble

10. In decision theory and estimation theory, the _____ of an estimator, $\hat{\theta}$, of an unknown parameter of the distribution, θ, is the expected value of the loss function

$$R(\theta, \hat{\theta}) = \mathbb{E}_\theta L(\theta, \hat{\theta}) = \int L(\theta, \hat{\theta})\, dP_\theta.$$

where dP_θ is a probability measure parametrized by θ.

- For a scalar parameter θ and a quadratic loss function,

$$L(\theta, \hat{\theta}) = (\theta - \hat{\theta})^2$$

the _____ function becomes the mean squared error of the estimate,

$$R(\theta, \hat{\theta}) = E_\theta(\theta - \hat{\theta})^2$$

- In density estimation, the unknown parameter is probability density itself. The loss function is typically chosen to be a norm in an appropriate function space. For example, for L^2 norm,

$$L(f, \hat{f}) = \|f - \hat{f}\|_2^2$$

the _____ function becomes the mean integrated squared error

$$R(f, \hat{f}) = E\|f - \hat{f}\|^2$$

a. Linear model
b. Risk
c. Risk aversion
d. Financial modeling

11. An _____ is a person who has possession of an enterprise and assumes significant accountability for the inherent risks and the outcome. It is an ambitious leader who combines land, labor, and capital to create and market new goods or services. The term is a loanword from French and was first defined by the Irish economist Richard Cantillon.
a. A Stake in the Outcome
b. A4e
c. AAAI
d. Entrepreneur

12. _____ is an idea in the field of Organizational studies and management which describes the psychology, attitudes, experiences, beliefs and Values (personal and cultural values) of an organization. It has been defined as 'the specific collection of values and norms that are shared by people and groups in an organization and that control the way they interact with each other and with stakeholders outside the organization.'

Chapter 6. Managing Change: Innovation and Diversity   57

This definition continues to explain organizational values also known as 'beliefs and ideas about what kinds of goals members of an organization should pursue and ideas about the appropriate kinds or standards of behavior organizational members should use to achieve these goals. From organizational values develop organizational norms, guidelines or expectations that prescribe appropriate kinds of behavior by employees in particular situations and control the behavior of organizational members towards one another.'

_____ is not the same as corporate culture.

a. Union shop
b. Organizational effectiveness
c. Organizational development
d. Organizational culture

13. An _____ is a mostly hierarchical concept of subordination of entities that collaborate and contribute to serve one common aim.

Organizations are a variant of clustered entities. The structure of an organization is usually set up in many a styles, dependent on their objectives and ambience.

a. Organizational development
b. Organizational structure
c. Open shop
d. Informal organization

14. Engineering _____ is the permissible limit of variation in

1. a physical dimension,
2. a measured value or physical property of a material, manufactured object, system, or service,
3. other measured values (such as temperature, humidity, etc.)
4. in engineering and safety, a physical distance or space (_____), as in a truck (lorry), train or boat under a bridge as well as a train in a tunnel

Dimensions, properties, or conditions may vary within certain practical limits without significantly affecting functioning of equipment or a process. _____s are specified to allow reasonable leeway for imperfections and inherent variability without compromising performance.

The _____ may be specified as a factor or percentage of the nominal value, a maximum deviation from a nominal value, an explicit range of allowed values, be specified by a note or published standard with this information, or be implied by the numeric accuracy of the nominal value. _____ can be symmetrical, as in 40±0.1, or asymmetrical, such as 40+0.2/−0.1.

a. Quality assurance
b. Zero defects
c. Root cause analysis
d. Tolerance

15.

The terms _____ and positive action refer to policies that take race, ethnicity, or gender into consideration in an attempt to promote equal opportunity. The focus of such policies ranges from employment and education to public contracting and health programs. The impetus towards _____ is twofold: to maximize diversity in all levels of society, along with its presumed benefits, and to redress perceived disadvantages due to overt, institutional, or involuntary discrimination.

a. Abraham Harold Maslow
b. Adam Smith
c. Affirmative action
d. Affiliation

16. The 'business case for _____', theorizes that in a global marketplace, a company that employs a diverse workforce (both men and women, people of many generations, people from ethnically and racially diverse backgrounds etc.) is better able to understand the demographics of the marketplace it serves and is thus better equipped to thrive in that marketplace than a company that has a more limited range of employee demographics.

An additional corollary suggests that a company that supports the _____ of its workforce can also improve employee satisfaction, productivity and retention.

a. Kanban
b. Trademark
c. Virtual team
d. Diversity

17. _____ is a concept in ethics with several meanings. It is often used synonymously with such concepts as responsibility, answerability, enforcement, blameworthiness, liability and other terms associated with the expectation of account-giving. As an aspect of governance, it has been central to discussions related to problems in both the public and private (corporation) worlds.

a. A Stake in the Outcome
b. Usury
c. A4e
d. Accountability

18. In economics, the term _____ refers to situations where the advancement of a qualified person within the hierarchy of an organization is stopped at a lower level because of some form of discrimination, most commonly sexism or racism, but since the term was coined, '_____' has also come to describe the limited advancement of the deaf, blind, disabled, aged and sexual minorities.It is an unofficial, invisible barrier that prevents women and minorities from advancing in businesses.

This situation is referred to as a 'ceiling' as there is a limitation blocking upward advancement, and 'glass' (transparent) because the limitation is not immediately apparent and is normally an unwritten and unofficial policy. This invisible barrier continues to exist, even though there are no explicit obstacles keeping minorities from acquiring advanced job positions - there are no advertisements that specifically say 'no minorities hired at this establishment', nor are there any formal orders that say 'minorities are not qualified' - but they do lie beneath the surface.

a. 28-hour day
b. 33 Strategies of War
c. Glass ceiling
d. 1990 Clean Air Act

19. There are two types of _____ relationships: formal and informal. Informal relationships develop on their own between partners. Formal _____, on the other hand, refers to assigned relationships, often associated with organizational _____ programs designed to promote employee development or to assist at-risk children and youth.
a. Fix it twice
b. Human resource management system
c. Real Property Administrator
d. Mentoring

20. _____ is unwelcome harassment of a sexual nature, or based upon the receiving party's sex or gender. In some contexts or circumstances, _____ may be illegal. It includes a range of behavior from seemingly mild transgressions and annoyances to actual sexual abuse or sexual assault.
a. Sexual harassment
b. Hypernorms
c. 28-hour day
d. 1990 Clean Air Act

Chapter 6. Managing Change: Innovation and Diversity

21. A _____ is the term given to a company that facilitates the learning of its members and continuously transforms itself. _____s develop as a result of the pressures facing modern organizations and enables them to remain competitive in the business environment. A _____ has five main features; systems thinking, personal mastery, mental models, shared vision and team learning.
   a. 1990 Clean Air Act
   b. Hoshin Kanri
   c. Quality function deployment
   d. Learning organization

22. _____ is an increasingly broadening term with which an organization, or other human system describes the combination of traditionally administrative personnel functions with acquisition and application of skills, knowledge and experience, Employee Relations and resource planning at various levels. The field draws upon concepts developed in Industrial/Organizational Psychology and System Theory. _____ has at least two related interpretations depending on context. The original usage derives from political economy and economics, where it was traditionally called labor, one of four factors of production although this perspective is changing as a function of new and ongoing research into more strategic approaches at national levels. This first usage is used more in terms of '_____ development', and can go beyond just organizations to the level of nations . The more traditional usage within corporations and businesses refers to the individuals within a firm or agency, and to the portion of the organization that deals with hiring, firing, training, and other personnel issues, typically referred to as `_____ management'.
   a. Progressive discipline
   b. Bradford Factor
   c. Human resource management
   d. Human resources

23. As defined by Richard Beckhard, _____ is a planned, top-down, organization-wide effort to increase the organization's effectiveness and health. _____ is achieved through interventions in the organization's 'processes,' using behavioural science knowledge. According to Warren Bennis, _____ is a complex strategy intended to change the beliefs, attitudes, values, and structure of organizations so that they can better adapt to new technologies, markets, and challenges.
   a. Organizational development
   b. Organizational structure
   c. Organizational culture
   d. Informal organization

24. Levi Strauss, born Löb Strauss (February 26, 1829 - September 26, 1902) was a German-Jewish immigrant to the United States who founded the first company to manufacture blue jeans. His firm, _____, began in 1853 in San Francisco, California.

Levi Strauss was born in Bavaria, Germany, to Hirsch Strauss and his wife Rebecca (Haas) Strauss.

Chapter 6. Managing Change: Innovation and Diversity 61

a. Abraham Harold Maslow
b. Adam Smith
c. Affiliation
d. Levi Strauss ' Company

25. _____ is a form of training that claims to make people more aware of their own prejudices, and more sensitive to others. According to its critics, it involves the use of psychological techniques with groups that its critics claim are often identical to brainwashing tactics. Critics believe these techniques are unethical.

a. 1990 Clean Air Act
b. 28-hour day
c. 33 Strategies of War
d. Sensitivity training

26. _____ is an influential development in the field of social science. It provides a framework for looking at the factors (forces) that influence a situation, originally social situations. It looks at forces that are either driving movement toward a goal (helping forces) or blocking movement toward a goal (hindering forces.)

a. Dynamic Enterprise Modeling
b. Force field Analysis
c. Logistics management
d. Board of governors

27. _____ describes the situation when output from (or information about the result of) an event or phenomenon in the past will influence the same event/phenomenon in the present or future. When an event is part of a chain of cause-and-effect that forms a circuit or loop, then the event is said to 'feed back' into itself.

_____ is also a synonym for:

- _____ signal; the information about the initial event that is the basis for subsequent modification of the event.
- _____ loop; the causal path that leads from the initial generation of the _____ signal to the subsequent modification of the event.

_____ is a mechanism, process or signal that is looped back to control a system within itself. Such a loop is called a _____ loop.

Chapter 6. Managing Change: Innovation and Diversity

a. Feedback
b. Positive feedback
c. Feedback loop
d. 1990 Clean Air Act

28. In organizational development (OD), _____ is the application of Socio-Technical Systems principles and techniques to the humanization of work.

The aims of _____ to improved job satisfaction, to improved through-put, to improved quality and to reduced employee problems, e.g., grievances, absenteeism.

Under scientific management people would be directed by reason and the problems of industrial unrest would be appropriately (i.e., scientifically) addressed.

a. Graduate recruitment
b. Work design
c. Path-goal theory
d. Management process

29. A _____ is one of several ways of doing research whether it is social science related or even socially related. It is an intensive study of a single group, incident, or community. Other ways include experiments, surveys, multiple histories, and analysis of archival information.

Rather than using samples and following a rigid protocol to examine limited number of variables, _____ methods involve an in-depth, longitudinal examination of a single instance or event: a case.

a. Case study
b. Longitudinal study
c. Standard operating procedure
d. 1990 Clean Air Act

Chapter 7. Human Resources Management 63

1. _____ is an increasingly broadening term with which an organization, or other human system describes the combination of traditionally administrative personnel functions with acquisition and application of skills, knowledge and experience, Employee Relations and resource planning at various levels. The field draws upon concepts developed in Industrial/Organizational Psychology and System Theory. _____ has at least two related interpretations depending on context. The original usage derives from political economy and economics, where it was traditionally called labor, one of four factors of production although this perspective is changing as a function of new and ongoing research into more strategic approaches at national levels. This first usage is used more in terms of '_____ development', and can go beyond just organizations to the level of nations . The more traditional usage within corporations and businesses refers to the individuals within a firm or agency, and to the portion of the organization that deals with hiring, firing, training, and other personnel issues, typically referred to as `_____ management'.
    a. Human resource management
    b. Human resources
    c. Progressive discipline
    d. Bradford Factor

2. _____ is a process of planning and controlling the performance or execution of any type of activity, such as:

    - a project (project _____) or
    - a process (process _____, sometimes referred to as the process performance measurement and management system.)

Organization's senior management is responsible for carrying out its _____.

    a. Human Relations Movement
    b. Work design
    c. Participatory management
    d. Management process

3. The _____ was a landmark piece of legislation in the United States that outlawed racial segregation in schools, public places, and employment.
    a. Civil Rights Act of 1964
    b. Financial Security Law of France
    c. Design patent
    d. Negligence in employment

4. _____ is a contract between two parties, one being the employer and the other being the employee. An employee may be defined as: 'A person in the service of another under any contract of hire, express or implied, oral or written, where the employer has the power or right to control and direct the employee in the material details of how the work is to be performed.' Black's Law Dictionary page 471 (5th ed. 1979.)

Chapter 7. Human Resources Management

a. Exit interview
b. Employment counsellor
c. Employment rate
d. Employment

5. The term _____ was created by President Lyndon B. Johnson when he signed Executive Order 11246 on September 24, 1965, created to prohibit federal contractors from discriminating against employees on the basis of race, sex, creed, religion, color, or national origin. In more recent times, most employers have also added sexual orientation to the list of non-discrimination.

The Executive Order also required contractors to implement affirmative action plans to increase the participation of minorities and women in the workplace.

a. A4e
b. AAAI
c. A Stake in the Outcome
d. Equal Employment Opportunity

6. The U.S. _____ is a federal agency whose goal is ending employment discrimination. The _____ investigates discrimination complaints based on an individual's race, color, national origin, religion, sex, age, disability and retaliation for reporting and/or opposing a discriminatory practice. The Commission is also tasked with filing suits on behalf of alleged victim(s) of discrimination against employers and as an adjudicatory for claims of discrimination brought against federal agencies.

a. ARCO
b. Airbus SAS
c. Airbus Industrie
d. Equal Employment Opportunity Commission

7. In employment law, a (BFOQ) (US) or bona fide occupational requirement (BFOR) (Canada) is a quality or an attribute that employers are allowed to consider when making decisions on the hiring and retention of employees - qualities that, when considered, in other contexts would be considered discriminatory and thus violating civil rights employment law.

In employment discrimination law in the United States, United States Code Title 29 , Chapter 14 (age discrimination in employment), section 623 (prohibition of age discrimination) establishes that 'It shall not be unlawful for an employer, employment agency, or labor organization (1) to take any action otherwise prohibited under subsections (a), (b), (c), or (e) of this section where age is a _____ reasonably necessary to the normal operation of the particular business, or where the differentiation is based on reasonable factors other than age, or where such practices involve an employee in a workplace in a foreign country, and compliance with such subsections would cause such employer, or a corporation controlled by such employer, to violate the laws of the country in which such workplace is located.'

One example of _____s are mandatory retirement ages for bus drivers and airline pilots, for safety reasons. Further, in advertising, a manufacturer of men's clothing may lawfully advertise for male models.

a. Sick leave
b. Corporate governance
c. MacPherson v. Buick Motor Co.
d. Bona fide occupational qualification

8. _____ refers to various methodologies for analyzing the requirements of a job.

The general purpose of _____ is to document the requirements of a job and the work performed. Job and task analysis is performed as a basis for later improvements, including: definition of a job domain; describing a job; developing performance appraisals, selection systems, promotion criteria, training needs assessment, and compensation plans.

a. Management process
b. Hersey-Blanchard situational theory
c. Work design
d. Job Analysis

9. _____ is an internal recruitment method employed by organisations to identify potential candidates from their existing employees social networks. An _____ scheme encourages a company's existing employees to select and recruit the suitable candidates from their social networks. As a reward, the employer typically pays the referring employee a referral bonus.

a. Employee referral
b. Executive search
c. Employment agency
d. Internet recruiting

10. A _____ represents the mutual beliefs, perceptions, and informal obligations between an employer and an employee. It sets the dynamics for the relationship and defines the detailed practicality of the work to be done. It is distinguishable from the formal written contract of employment which, for the most part, only identifies mutual duties and responsibilities in a generalized form.

a. Spatial mismatch
b. Career
c. Psychological contract
d. Skilled worker

11. _____ is an advertisement in which a particular product specifically mentions a competitor by name for the express purpose of showing why the competitor is inferior to the product naming it.

This should not be confused with parody advertisements, where a fictional product is being advertised for the purpose of poking fun at the particular advertisement, nor should it be confused with the use of a coined brand name for the purpose of comparing the product without actually naming an actual competitor. ('Wikipedia tastes better and is less filling than the Encyclopedia Galactica.')

In the 1980s, during what has been referred to as the cola wars, soft-drink manufacturer Pepsi ran a series of advertisements where people, caught on hidden camera, in a blind taste test, chose Pepsi over rival Coca-Cola.

   a. 33 Strategies of War
   b. 1990 Clean Air Act
   c. 28-hour day
   d. Comparative advertising

12. A _____ is someone engaging in recruitment, which is the solicitation of individuals to fill jobs or positions within any group, such as a corporation or sports team. _____s can be divided into two groups; those working internally for one organization, and those working for multiple clients in a third-party broker relationship, sometimes called headhunters or agency _____s.

An internal _____ is member of a company or organization and typically works in human resources (HR), which in the past was known as the Personnel Office, or just Personnel.

   a. 1990 Clean Air Act
   b. 28-hour day
   c. Recruiter
   d. 33 Strategies of War

13. A _____ or background investigation is the process of looking up and compiling criminal records, commercial records and financial records (in certain instances such as employment screening) of an individual.

_____s are often requested by employers on job candidates, especially on candidates seeking a position that requires high security or a position of trust, such as in a school, hospital, financial institution, airport, and government (including law enforcement and military.) These checks are traditionally administered by a government agency for a nominal fee, but can also be administered by private companies.

Chapter 7. Human Resources Management

a. Malcolm Baldrige National Quality Award
b. Time and attendance
c. Labour productivity
d. Background check

14. _____-model (SCOR(r)) is a process reference model developed by the management consulting firm PRTM and AMR Research and endorsed by the Supply-Chain Council (SCC) as the cross-industry de facto standard diagnostic tool for supply chain management. SCOR enables users to address, improve, and communicate supply chain management practices within and between all interested parties in the Extended Enterprise.

SCOR(r) is a management tool, spanning from the supplier's supplier to the customer's customer. The model has been developed by the members of the Council on a volunteer basis to describe the business activities associated with all phases of satisfying a customer's demand.

a. Supply-Chain Operations Reference
b. Supply Chain Risk Management
c. Delayed differentiation
d. Supply chain management software

15. The 'business case for _____', theorizes that in a global marketplace, a company that employs a diverse workforce (both men and women, people of many generations, people from ethnically and racially diverse backgrounds etc.) is better able to understand the demographics of the marketplace it serves and is thus better equipped to thrive in that marketplace than a company that has a more limited range of employee demographics.

An additional corollary suggests that a company that supports the _____ of its workforce can also improve employee satisfaction, productivity and retention.

a. Virtual team
b. Kanban
c. Trademark
d. Diversity

16. A _____ is a quantitative research method commonly employed in survey research. The aim of this approach is to ensure that each interviewee is presented with exactly the same questions in the same order. This ensures that answers can be reliably aggregated and that comparisons can be made with confidence between sample subgroups or between different survey periods.

a. Questionnaire construction
b. Structured interview
c. Questionnaire
d. Mystery shoppers

17. _____ are a method of interviews where questions can be changed or adapted to meet the respondent's intelligence, understanding or belief. Unlike a structured interview they do not offer a limited, pre-set range of answers for a respondent to choose, but instead advocate listening to how each individual person responds to the question.

The method to gather information using this technique is fairly limited, for example most surveys that are carried out via telephone or even in person tend to follow a structured method.

a. AAAI
b. A4e
c. A Stake in the Outcome
d. Unstructured interviews

18. A _____ is an alliance among individuals or groups, during which they cooperate in joint action, each in his own self-interest, joining forces together for a common cause. This alliance may be temporary or a matter of convenience. A _____ thus differs from a more formal covenant.

a. 33 Strategies of War
b. 1990 Clean Air Act
c. 28-hour day
d. Coalition

19. The _____ refers to a cognitive bias whereby the perception of a particular trait is influenced by the perception of the former traits in a sequence of interpretations.

Edward L. Thorndike was the first to support the _____ with empirical research. In a psychology study published in 1920, Thorndike asked commanding officers to rate their soldiers; Thorndike found high cross-correlation between all positive and all negative traits.

a. Cognitive biases
b. Distinction bias
c. Sunk costs
d. Halo effect

Chapter 7. Human Resources Management

20. _____ is a method by which the job performance of an employee is evaluated _____ is a part of career development.

_____s are regular reviews of employee performance within organizations

Generally, the aims of a _____ are to:

- Give feedback on performance to employees.
- Identify employee training needs.
- Document criteria used to allocate organizational rewards.
- Form a basis for personnel decisions: salary increases, promotions, disciplinary actions, etc.
- Provide the opportunity for organizational diagnosis and development.
- Facilitate communication between employee and administraton
- Validate selection techniques and human resource policies to meet federal Equal Employment Opportunity requirements.

A common approach to assessing performance is to use a numerical or scalar rating system whereby managers are asked to score an individual against a number of objectives/attributes. In some companies, employees receive assessments from their manager, peers, subordinates and customers while also performing a self assessment.

a. Personnel management
b. Progressive discipline
c. Human resource management
d. Performance appraisal

21. In psychology research on behaviorism, _____ are scales used to report performance. _____ are normally presented vertically with scale points ranging from five to nine.

It is an appraisal method that aims to combine the benefits of narratives, critical incident incidents, and quantified ratings by anchoring a quantified scale with specific narrative examples of good or poor performance.

a. 1990 Clean Air Act
b. 33 Strategies of War
c. 28-hour day
d. Behaviorally anchored rating scales

22. The _____ is a trilateral trade bloc in North America created by the governments of the United States, Canada, and Mexico. The agreement creating the trade bloc came into force on January 1, 1994. It superseded the Canada-United States Free Trade Agreement between the U.S. and Canada.

a. Trade union
b. Business war game
c. North American Free Trade Agreement
d. Career portfolios

23. A _____ is a set of categories designed to elicit information about a quantitative or a qualitative attribute. In the social sciences, common examples are the Likert scale and 1-10 _____s in which a person selects the number which is considered to reflect the perceived quality of a product.

A _____ is an instrument that requires the rater to assign the rated object that have numerals assigned to them.

a. Polytomous Rasch model
b. Spearman-Brown prediction formula
c. Thurstone scale
d. Rating Scale

24. A _____ is a compensation, usually financial, received by a worker in exchange for their labor.

Compensation in terms of _____s is given to worker and compensation in terms of salary is given to employees. Compensation is a monetary benefits given to employees in returns of the services provided by them.

a. Wage
b. Profit-sharing agreement
c. State Compensation Insurance Fund
d. Performance-related pay

25. In economics and sociology, an _____ is any factor (financial or non-financial) that enables or motivates a particular course of action, or counts as a reason for preferring one choice to the alternatives. It is an expectation that encourages people to behave in a certain way. Since human beings are purposeful creatures, the study of _____ structures is central to the study of all economic activity (both in terms of individual decision-making and in terms of co-operation and competition within a larger institutional structure.)
a. Incentive
b. A Stake in the Outcome
c. A4e
d. AAAI

Chapter 7. Human Resources Management

26. In general, a _____ is an arrangement to provide people with an income when they are no longer earning a regular income from employment.

The terms retirement plan or superannuation refer to a _____ granted upon retirement. Retirement plans may be set up by employers, insurance companies, the government or other institutions such as employer associations or trade unions.

   a. State Compensation Insurance Fund
   b. Wage
   c. Pension
   d. Pension insurance contract

27. Piece work or piecework describes types of employment in which a worker is paid a fixed '_____' for each unit produced or action performed. Piece work is also a form of performance-related pay (Piece rateP) and is the oldest form of performance pay.

In a manufacturing setting, the output of piece work can be measured by the number of physical items (pieces) produced, such as when a garment worker is paid per operational step completed, regardless of the time required.

   a. Piece rate
   b. Piecework
   c. Scientific management
   d. Methods-time measurement

28. _____, when used as a special term, refers to various incentive plans introduced by businesses that provide direct or indirect payments to employees that depend on company's profitability in addition to employees' regular salary and bonuses. In publicly traded companies these plans typically amount to allocation of shares to employees.

The _____ plans are based on predetermined economic sharing rules that define the split of gains between the company as a principal and the employee as an agent.

   a. Federal Wage System
   b. Living wage
   c. Wage
   d. Profit sharing

29. _____ occurs when a person is available to work and seeking work but currently without work. The prevalence of _____ is usually measured using the _____ rate, which is defined as the percentage of those in the labor force who are unemployed. The _____ rate is also used in economic studies and economic indexes such as the United States' Conference Board's Index of Leading Indicators as a measure of the state of the macroeconomics.
   a. Unemployment
   b. Outplacement
   c. Unemployment Convention, 1919
   d. Employment-to-population ratio

30. _____ is money received by an unemployed worker from the United States or a state. In the United States, this compensation is classified as a type of social welfare benefit. According to the Internal Revenue Code, these types of benefits are to be included in a taxpayer's gross income.
   a. Unemployment compensation
   b. Unemployment insurance
   c. Unemployment Provision Convention, 1934
   d. Unemployment

31. _____ is a concept in ethics with several meanings. It is often used synonymously with such concepts as responsibility, answerability, enforcement, blameworthiness, liability and other terms associated with the expectation of account-giving. As an aspect of governance, it has been central to discussions related to problems in both the public and private (corporation) worlds.
   a. A Stake in the Outcome
   b. A4e
   c. Usury
   d. Accountability

32. The field of _____ looks at the relationship between management and workers, particularly groups of workers represented by a union.

   _____ is an important factor in analyzing 'varieties of capitalism', such as neocorporatism, social democracy, and neoliberalism

   a. Organizational effectiveness
   b. Informal organization
   c. Industrial relations
   d. Overtime

33.

Chapter 7. Human Resources Management 73

Founded in 1958 by Dr. Charles Kepner and Dr. Benjamin Tregoe, _____, Inc., is a global organisation providing consulting and training services around problem solving, decision making and project execution methodologies.

_____'s trademark technique, Rational Process, which is commonly referred to as the 'KT Process', is the creation of structured, systematic processes which are used to maximise the critical thinking skills of key stakeholders in a particular situation, problem (potential or real), decision or opportunity.

The Rational Processes are broken down into the following:SITUATION APPRAISAL - the process of ensuring that priority and order are established for multiple concerns associated with a specific issue.Example - The company's in-house built payroll system is becoming outdated and increasingly difficult to support.

 a. Kepner-Tregoe
 b. Hierarchical Decision Process
 c. Multi-Criteria Decision Analysis
 d. Multi-Attribute Global Inference of Quality

34. The _____ is a 1935 United States federal law that limits the means with which employers may react to workers in the private sector that organize labor unions, engage in collective bargaining, and take part in strikes and other forms of concerted activity in support of their demands. The Act does not, on the other hand, cover those workers who are covered by the Railway Labor Act, agricultural employees, domestic employees, supervisors, independent contractors and some close relatives of individual employers.

It was in a context of severe economic troubles that the Wagner Act came into effect.

 a. 33 Strategies of War
 b. 28-hour day
 c. 1990 Clean Air Act
 d. National Labor Relations Act

35. _____ is a cross-disciplinary area concerned with protecting the safety, health and welfare of people engaged in work or employment. The goal of all _____ programs is to foster a work free safe environment. As a secondary effect, it may also protect co-workers, family members, employers, customers, suppliers, nearby communities, and other members of the public who are impacted by the workplace environment.
 a. A4e
 b. Occupational Safety and Health
 c. A Stake in the Outcome
 d. AAAI

Chapter 7. Human Resources Management

36. The United States _____ is an agency of the United States Department of Labor. It was created by Congress under the Occupational Safety and Health Act, signed by President Richard M. Nixon, on December 29, 1970. Its mission is to prevent work-related injuries, illnesses, and deaths by issuing and enforcing rules (called standards) for workplace safety and health.
    a. Opinion leadership
    b. Unemployment insurance
    c. Operant conditioning
    d. Occupational Safety and Health Administration

37. A _____ is a working environment with conditions that are considered by many people of industrialized nations to be difficult or dangerous, usually where the workers have few opportunities to address their situation. This can include exposure to harmful materials, hazardous situations, extreme temperatures, or abuse from employers. _____ workers often work long hours for little pay, regardless of any laws mandating overtime pay or a minimum wage.
    a. Continuous
    b. Rate of return
    c. Sweatshop
    d. Complement

38. An arbitral tribunal (or arbitration tribunal) is a panel of one or more adjudicators which is convened and sits to resolve a dispute by way of arbitration. The tribunal may consist of a sole _____, or there may be two or more _____s, which might include either a chairman or an umpire. The parties to a dispute are usually free to agree the number and composition of the arbitral tribunal.
    a. A Stake in the Outcome
    b. Arbitrator
    c. AAAI
    d. A4e

39. In organized labor, _____ is the method whereby workers organize together (usually in unions) to meet, converse, and negotiate upon the work conditions with their employers normally resulting in a written contract setting forth the wages, hours, and other conditions to be observed for a stipulated period.It is the practice in which union and company representatives meet to negotiate a new labor contract. In various national labor and employment law contexts, the term _____ takes on a more specific legal meaning. In a broad sense, however, it is the coming together of workers to negotiate their employment.
    a. Labor rights
    b. Labour law
    c. Paid time off
    d. Collective bargaining

Chapter 7. Human Resources Management

40. _____, a form of alternative dispute resolution (ADR) or 'appropriate dispute resolution', aims to assist two (or more) disputants in reaching an agreement. The parties themselves determine the conditions of any settlements reached-- rather than accepting something imposed by a third party. The disputes may involve (as parties) states, organizations, communities, individuals or other representatives with a vested interest in the outcome.
  a. Foreign Corrupt Practices Act
  b. Meritor Savings Bank v. Vinson
  c. Maximum medical improvement
  d. Mediation

41. An _____ is an interview conducted by an employer of a departing employee. They are generally conducted by a relatively neutral party, such as a human resources staff member, so that the employee will be more inclined to be candid, as opposed to worrying about burning bridges. For this reason, some companies opt to employ a third party to conduct the interviews and provide feedback.
  a. Exit interview
  b. Extra role performance
  c. Underemployment
  d. Occupational Employment Statistics

42. _____ is the temporary suspension or permanent termination of employment of an employee or (more commonly) a group of employees for business reasons, such as the decision that certain positions are no longer necessary or a business slow-down or interruption in work. Originally the term '_____' referred exclusively to a temporary interruption in work, as when factory work cyclically falls off. However, in recent times the term can also refer to the permanent elimination of a position.
  a. Wrongful dismissal
  b. Retirement
  c. Termination of employment
  d. Layoff

43. _____ is a term used to describe the efforts made by a downsizing company to help its redundant employees through the redundancy transition and help them re-orientate to the job market . A consultancy firm usually provides the _____ services. This is achieved through practical and psychological support.
  a. Unemployment Provision Convention, 1934
  b. Unemployment compensation
  c. Unemployment benefits
  d. Outplacement

44. A _____ is one of several ways of doing research whether it is social science related or even socially related. It is an intensive study of a single group, incident, or community. Other ways include experiments, surveys, multiple histories, and analysis of archival information .

Rather than using samples and following a rigid protocol to examine limited number of variables, _____ methods involve an in-depth, longitudinal examination of a single instance or event: a case.

   a. 1990 Clean Air Act
   b. Standard operating procedure
   c. Longitudinal study
   d. Case study

45. _____ is a term defined by the Oxford English Dictionary as an individual's 'course or progress through life '. It is usually considered to pertain to remunerative work (and sometimes also formal education.)

The etymology of the term is somewhat ironic in that it comes from the Latin word carrera, which means race .

   a. Nursing shortage
   b. Career
   c. Career planning
   d. Spatial mismatch

46. A _____ or covering letter or motivation letter or motivational letter or letter of motivation is a letter of introduction attached to, or accompanying another document such as a résumé or curriculum vitae.

Job seekers frequently send résumés or employment applications as attachments to a _____, by way of introducing themselves to recruiters or prospective employers and indicating their interest in the positions. Employers may look for individualized and thoughtfully written _____s to screen applicants who are not sufficiently interested in their position or who lack the required writing skills.

   a. Job fraud
   b. Work-at-home scheme
   c. Per diem
   d. Cover letter

47. A _____ is a process in which a potential employee is evaluated by an employer for prospective employment in their company, organization and was established in the late 16th century.

A _____ typically precedes the hiring decision, and is used to evaluate the candidate. The interview is usually preceded by the evaluation of submitted résumés from interested candidates, then selecting a small number of candidates for interviews.

a. Payrolling
b. Supported employment
c. Split shift
d. Job Interview

Chapter 8. Organizational Behavior: Power, Politics, Conflict, and Stress

1. In psychology, _____ is a major approach to the study of human personality. Trait theorists are primarily interested in the measurement of traits, which can be defined as habitual patterns of behavior, thought, and emotion. According to this perspective, traits are relatively stable over time, differ among individuals (e.g. some people are outgoing whereas others are shy), and influence behavior.
   a. Trait theory
   b. Psychometrics
   c. Psychological statistics
   d. Cognitive dissonance

2. _____ is one of the managerial functions like planning, organizing, staffing and directing. It is an important function because it helps to check the errors and to take the corrective action so that deviation from standards are minimized and stated goals of the organization are achieved in desired manner. According to modern concepts, _____ is a foreseeing action whereas earlier concept of _____ was used only when errors were detected. _____ in management means setting standards, measuring actual performance and taking corrective action.
   a. Schedule of reinforcement
   b. Decision tree pruning
   c. Turnover
   d. Control

3. _____ is a term in psychology which refers to a person's belief about what causes the good or bad results in his or her life, either in general or in a specific area such as health or academics. Understanding of the concept was developed by Julian B. Rotter in 1954, and has since become an important aspect of personality studies.

   _____ refers to the extent to which individuals believe that they can control events that affect them.

   a. Social loafing
   b. Machiavellianism
   c. Self-enhancement
   d. Locus of control

4. _____ is, according to the OED, 'the employment of cunning and duplicity in statecraft or in general conduct', deriving from the Italian Renaissance diplomat and writer Niccolò Machiavelli, who wrote Il Principe and other works. Machiavellian and variants became very popular in the late 16th century in English, though '_____' itself is first cited by the OED from 1626. The word has a similar use in modern psychology.
   a. Personal space
   b. Persuasion
   c. Self-enhancement
   d. Machiavellianism

Chapter 8. Organizational Behavior: Power, Politics, Conflict, and Stress 79

5. In decision theory and estimation theory, the _____ of an estimator, $\hat{\theta}$, of an unknown parameter of the distribution, θ, is the expected value of the loss function

$$R(\theta, \hat{\theta}) = \mathbb{E}_\theta L(\theta, \hat{\theta}) = \int L(\theta, \hat{\theta})\, dP_\theta.$$

where dP_θ is a probability measure parametrized by θ.

- For a scalar parameter θ and a quadratic loss function,

$$L(\theta, \hat{\theta}) = (\theta - \hat{\theta})^2$$

the _____ function becomes the mean squared error of the estimate,

$$R(\theta, \hat{\theta}) = E_\theta (\theta - \hat{\theta})^2$$

- In density estimation, the unknown parameter is probability density itself. The loss function is typically chosen to be a norm in an appropriate function space. For example, for L^2 norm,

$$L(f, \hat{f}) = \|f - \hat{f}\|_2^2$$

the _____ function becomes the mean integrated squared error

$$R(f, \hat{f}) = E\|f - \hat{f}\|^2$$

a. Financial modeling
b. Linear model
c. Risk aversion
d. Risk

6. _____ is one of five major domains of personality discovered by psychologists. Openness involves active imagination, aesthetic sensitivity, attentiveness to inner feelings, preference for variety, and intellectual curiosity. A great deal of psychometric research has demonstrated that these qualities are statistically correlated.

a. Introverts
b. Extraversion
c. Introversion
d. Openness to experience

7. _____ is the belief that one is capable of performing in a certain manner to attain certain goals. It is a belief that one has the capabilities to execute the courses of actions required to manage prospective situations. Unlike efficacy, which is the power to produce an effect (in essence, competence), _____ is the belief (whether or not accurate) that one has the power to produce that effect.
   a. 28-hour day
   b. 33 Strategies of War
   c. 1990 Clean Air Act
   d. Self-efficacy

8. In psychology, _____ reflects a person's overall evaluation or appraisal of his or her own worth.

_____ encompasses beliefs (for example, 'I am competent/incompetent') and emotions (for example, triumph/despair, pride/shame.) Behavior may reflect _____

   a. 28-hour day
   b. 33 Strategies of War
   c. 1990 Clean Air Act
   d. Self-esteem

9. A _____ is a prediction that directly or indirectly causes itself to become true, by the very terms of the prophecy itself, due to positive feedback between belief and behavior. Although examples of such prophecies can be found in literature as far back as ancient Greece and ancient India, it is 20th-century sociologist Robert K. Merton who is credited with coining the expression '_____' and formalizing its structure and consequences. In his book Social Theory and Social Structure, Merton gives as a feature of the _____:

In other words, a prophecy declared as truth when it is actually false may sufficiently influence people, either through fear or logical confusion, so that their reactions ultimately fulfill the once-false prophecy.

   a. 1990 Clean Air Act
   b. 28-hour day
   c. 33 Strategies of War
   d. Self-fulfilling prophecy

10. _____ describes how content an individual is with his or her job.

The happier people are within their job, the more satisfied they are said to be. _____ is not the same as motivation, although it is clearly linked.

   a. Human relations
   b. Goal-setting theory
   c. Job analysis
   d. Job satisfaction

11. _____ refers to increasing the spiritual, political, social or economic strength of individuals and communities. It often involves the empowered developing confidence in their own capacities.

The term Human _____ covers a vast landscape of meanings, interpretations, definitions and disciplines ranging from psychology and philosophy to the highly commercialized Self-Help industry and Motivational sciences.

   a. A4e
   b. Empowerment
   c. A Stake in the Outcome
   d. AAAI

12. _____ is individual power based on a high level of identification with, admiration of, or respect for the powerholder.

Nationalism, Patriotism, Celebrities and well-respected people are examples of _____ in effect.

_____ is one of the Five Bases of Social Power, as defined by Bertram Raven and his colleagues[1] in 1959.

   a. 28-hour day
   b. Referent power
   c. 1990 Clean Air Act
   d. 33 Strategies of War

13. A _____ is an alliance among individuals or groups, during which they cooperate in joint action, each in his own self-interest, joining forces together for a common cause. This alliance may be temporary or a matter of convenience. A _____ thus differs from a more formal covenant.

a. 33 Strategies of War
b. 1990 Clean Air Act
c. Coalition
d. 28-hour day

14. _____ refers to the long-term management of intractable conflicts. It is the label for the variety of ways by which people handle grievances--standing up for what they consider to be right and against what they consider to be wrong. Those ways include such diverse phenomena as gossip, ridicule, lynching, terrorism, warfare, feuding, genocide, law, mediation, and avoidance.
   a. 33 Strategies of War
   b. 28-hour day
   c. 1990 Clean Air Act
   d. Conflict Management

15. Various _____ can be employed dependent on the culture of the business, the nature of the task, the nature of the workforce and the personality and skills of the leaders. This idea was further developed by Robert Tannenbaum and Warren H. Schmidt (1958, 1973) who argued that the style of leadership is dependent upon the prevailing circumstance; therefore leaders should exercise a range of leadership styles and should deploy them as appropriate.

An Autocratic or authoritarian manager makes all the decisions, keeping the information and decision making among the senior management.

   a. 33 Strategies of War
   b. 28-hour day
   c. Management styles
   d. 1990 Clean Air Act

16. A _____ represents the mutual beliefs, perceptions, and informal obligations between an employer and an employee. It sets the dynamics for the relationship and defines the detailed practicality of the work to be done. It is distinguishable from the formal written contract of employment which, for the most part, only identifies mutual duties and responsibilities in a generalized form.
   a. Spatial mismatch
   b. Skilled worker
   c. Career
   d. Psychological contract

Chapter 8. Organizational Behavior: Power, Politics, Conflict, and Stress

17. In game theory and economic theory, _____ describes a situation in which a participant's gain or loss is exactly balanced by the losses or gains of the other participant(s.) If the total gains of the participants are added up, and the total losses are subtracted, they will sum to zero. _____ can be thought of more generally as constant sum where the benefits and losses to all players sum to the same value of money and pride and dignity.
    a. 33 Strategies of War
    b. 1990 Clean Air Act
    c. Zero-sum
    d. 28-hour day

18. _____ is a recursive process where two or more people or organizations work together in an intersection of common goals -- for example, an intellectual endeavor that is creative in nature--by sharing knowledge, learning and building consensus. _____ does not require leadership and can sometimes bring better results through decentralization and egalitarianism. In particular, teams that work collaboratively can obtain greater resources, recognition and reward when facing competition for finite resources._____ is also present in opposing goals exhibiting the notion of adversarial _____, though this is not a common case for using the term.
    a. Collaboration
    b. 1990 Clean Air Act
    c. 28-hour day
    d. Collectivism

19. _____ is a range of processes aimed at alleviating or eliminating sources of conflict. The term '_____' is sometimes used interchangeably with the term dispute resolution or alternative dispute resolution. Processes of _____ generally include negotiation, mediation and diplomacy.
    a. 28-hour day
    b. 33 Strategies of War
    c. Conflict resolution
    d. 1990 Clean Air Act

20. An arbitral tribunal (or arbitration tribunal) is a panel of one or more adjudicators which is convened and sits to resolve a dispute by way of arbitration. The tribunal may consist of a sole _____, or there may be two or more _____s, which might include either a chairman or an umpire. The parties to a dispute are usually free to agree the number and composition of the arbitral tribunal.
    a. AAAI
    b. A4e
    c. A Stake in the Outcome
    d. Arbitrator

21. _____, a form of alternative dispute resolution (ADR) or 'appropriate dispute resolution', aims to assist two (or more) disputants in reaching an agreement. The parties themselves determine the conditions of any settlements reached-- rather than accepting something imposed by a third party. The disputes may involve (as parties) states, organizations, communities, individuals or other representatives with a vested interest in the outcome.

a. Maximum medical improvement
b. Foreign Corrupt Practices Act
c. Meritor Savings Bank v. Vinson
d. Mediation

22. _____ is an idea in the field of Organizational studies and management which describes the psychology, attitudes, experiences, beliefs and Values (personal and cultural values) of an organization. It has been defined as 'the specific collection of values and norms that are shared by people and groups in an organization and that control the way they interact with each other and with stakeholders outside the organization.'

This definition continues to explain organizational values also known as 'beliefs and ideas about what kinds of goals members of an organization should pursue and ideas about the appropriate kinds or standards of behavior organizational members should use to achieve these goals. From organizational values develop organizational norms, guidelines or expectations that prescribe appropriate kinds of behavior by employees in particular situations and control the behavior of organizational members towards one another.'

_____ is not the same as corporate culture.

a. Union shop
b. Organizational effectiveness
c. Organizational development
d. Organizational culture

23. The _____ is a personality type theory that describes a pattern of behaviors that were once considered to be a risk factor for coronary heart disease. Since its inception in the 1950s, the theory has been widely popularized and also widely criticised for its scientific shortcomings.

Type A individuals can be described as impatient, excessively time-conscious, insecure about their status, highly competitive, over-ambitious, business-like, hostile, aggressive, incapable of relaxation in taking the smallest issues too seriously; and are somewhat disliked for the way that they're always rushing and demanding other people to serve to their standards of satisfaction.

a. 33 Strategies of War
b. 1990 Clean Air Act
c. Type A and Type B personality theory
d. 28-hour day

Chapter 8. Organizational Behavior: Power, Politics, Conflict, and Stress

24. _____ refers to a range of skills, tools, and techniques used to manage time when accomplishing specific tasks, projects and goals. This set encompass a wide scope of activities, and these include planning, allocating, setting goals, delegation, analysis of time spent, monitoring, organizing, scheduling, and prioritizing. Initially _____ referred to just business or work activities, but eventually the term broadened to include personal activities also.
   a. Cash cow
   b. Formula for Change
   c. Voice of the customer
   d. Time Management

25. _____ is a civil designation for persons who are incorporated in a fixed or permanent way to a society or group: regular member of the working staff, permanent staff distinguished from a supernumerary.

The term '_____' and its counterpart, 'supernumerary,' originated in Spanish and Latin American academy and government; it is now also used in countries all over the world, such as France, the U.S., England, Italy, etc.

There are _____ members of surgical organizations, of universities, of gastronomical associations, etc.

   a. Numerary
   b. Affiliation
   c. Adam Smith
   d. Abraham Harold Maslow

Chapter 9. Leading with Influence

1. _____ is a business magazine published by McGraw-Hill. It was first published in 1929 (as The Business Week) under the direction of Malcolm Muir, who was serving as president of the McGraw-Hill Publishing company at the time. Its primary competitors in the national business magazine category are Fortune and Forbes, which are published bi-weekly.

   a. The Wealth of Nations
   b. Democracy in America
   c. Hotel Vikas
   d. BusinessWeek

2. _____ has been described as the 'process of social influence in which one person can enlist the aid and support of others in the accomplishment of a common task'. A definition more inclusive of followers comes from Alan Keith of Genentech who said '_____ is ultimately about creating a way for people to contribute to making something extraordinary happen.'

   _____ is one of the most salient aspects of the organizational context. However, defining _____ has been challenging.

   a. Leadership
   b. 1990 Clean Air Act
   c. Situational leadership
   d. 28-hour day

3. _____ is an advertisement in which a particular product specifically mentions a competitor by name for the express purpose of showing why the competitor is inferior to the product naming it.

   This should not be confused with parody advertisements, where a fictional product is being advertised for the purpose of poking fun at the particular advertisement, nor should it be confused with the use of a coined brand name for the purpose of comparing the product without actually naming an actual competitor. ('Wikipedia tastes better and is less filling than the Encyclopedia Galactica.')

   In the 1980s, during what has been referred to as the cola wars, soft-drink manufacturer Pepsi ran a series of advertisements where people, caught on hidden camera, in a blind taste test, chose Pepsi over rival Coca-Cola.

   a. Comparative advertising
   b. 28-hour day
   c. 33 Strategies of War
   d. 1990 Clean Air Act

4. In psychology, _____ is a major approach to the study of human personality. Trait theorists are primarily interested in the measurement of traits, which can be defined as habitual patterns of behavior, thought, and emotion. According to this perspective, traits are relatively stable over time, differ among individuals (e.g. some people are outgoing whereas others are shy), and influence behavior.

a. Psychological statistics
b. Trait theory
c. Cognitive dissonance
d. Psychometrics

5. _____ is a term used to describe a policy of allowing events to take their own course. The term is a French phrase literally meaning 'let do'. It is a doctrine that states that government generally should not intervene in the marketplace.
   a. Libertarian
   b. Deep ecology
   c. Laissez-faire
   d. Freedom of contract

6. _____ refers to techniques, processes and tools for organizing and coordinating a group of individuals working towards a common goal--i.e. a team.

Several well-known approaches to _____ have come out of academic work. Examples include the Belbin Team Inventory by Meredith Belbin, a method to identify the different types of personalities within teams, and Ken Blanchard's description of 'High Performing Teams'.

   a. Team management
   b. 1990 Clean Air Act
   c. 33 Strategies of War
   d. 28-hour day

7. Various _____ can be employed dependent on the culture of the business, the nature of the task, the nature of the workforce and the personality and skills of the leaders. This idea was further developed by Robert Tannenbaum and Warren H. Schmidt (1958, 1973) who argued that the style of leadership is dependent upon the prevailing circumstance; therefore leaders should exercise a range of leadership styles and should deploy them as appropriate.

An Autocratic or authoritarian manager makes all the decisions, keeping the information and decision making among the senior management.

   a. 33 Strategies of War
   b. 28-hour day
   c. 1990 Clean Air Act
   d. Management styles

Chapter 9. Leading with Influence

8. The sociologist Max Weber defined _____ as 'resting on devotion to the exceptional sanctity, heroism or exemplary character of an individual person, and of the normative patterns or order revealed or ordained by him.' _____ is one of three forms of authority laid out in Weber's tripartite classification of authority, the other two being traditional authority and rational-legal authority. The concept has acquired wide usage among sociologists.

In his writings about _____, Weber applies the term charisma to 'a certain quality of an individual personality, by virtue of which he is set apart from ordinary men and treated as endowed with supernatural, superhuman, or at least specifically exceptional powers or qualities.

  a. Rational-legal authority
  b. Charismatic authority
  c. 28-hour day
  d. 1990 Clean Air Act

9. _____ is a term used to classify a group leadership theories that inquire the interactions between leaders and followers. A transactional leader focuses more on a series of 'transactions'. This person is interested in looking out for oneself, having exchange benefits with their subordinates and clarify a sense of duty with rewards and punishments to reach goals.
  a. 1990 Clean Air Act
  b. 33 Strategies of War
  c. 28-hour day
  d. Transactional leadership

10. _____ is a leadership style that defines as leadership that creates voluble and positive change in the followers. A transformational leader focuses on 'transforming' others to help each other, to look out for each other, be encouraging, harmonious, and look out for the organization as a whole. In this leadership, the leader enhances the motivation, moral and performance of his follower group.
  a. SESAMO
  b. Strong-Campbell Interest Inventory
  c. Polynomial conjoint measurement
  d. Transformational leadership

11. _____ is an approach to leadership development, coined and defined by Robert Greenleaf and advanced by several authors such as Stephen Covey, Peter Block, Peter Senge, Max DePree, Margaret Wheatley, Ken Blanchard, and others. Servant-leadership emphasizes the leader's role as steward of the resources (human, financial and otherwise) provided by the organization. It encourages leaders to serve others while staying focused on achieving results in line with the organization's values and integrity.

a. Servant leadership
b. Affiliation
c. Adam Smith
d. Abraham Harold Maslow

12. Contingency leadership theory in organizational studies is a type of leadership theory, leadership style, and leadership model that presumes that different leadership styles are contingent to different situations. It is also referred as _____ ® theory although, as originally convened, the situational theory term is much more restrictive. The original situational theory argues that the best type of leadership is totally determined by the situational variables.Currently there are many styles of leadership.
 a. Situational theory
 b. 1990 Clean Air Act
 c. Situational leadership
 d. 28-hour day

13. The 'business case for _____', theorizes that in a global marketplace, a company that employs a diverse workforce (both men and women, people of many generations, people from ethnically and racially diverse backgrounds etc.) is better able to understand the demographics of the marketplace it serves and is thus better equipped to thrive in that marketplace than a company that has a more limited range of employee demographics.

An additional corollary suggests that a company that supports the _____ of its workforce can also improve employee satisfaction, productivity and retention.

 a. Trademark
 b. Kanban
 c. Virtual team
 d. Diversity

14. A _____ is one of several ways of doing research whether it is social science related or even socially related. It is an intensive study of a single group, incident, or community.Other ways include experiments, surveys, multiple histories, and analysis of archival information .

Rather than using samples and following a rigid protocol to examine limited number of variables, _____ methods involve an in-depth, longitudinal examination of a single instance or event: a case.

a. Standard operating procedure
b. Case study
c. 1990 Clean Air Act
d. Longitudinal study

15. The _____ is a personality type theory that describes a pattern of behaviors that were once considered to be a risk factor for coronary heart disease. Since its inception in the 1950s, the theory has been widely popularized and also widely criticised for its scientific shortcomings.

Type A individuals can be described as impatient, excessively time-conscious, insecure about their status, highly competitive, over-ambitious, business-like, hostile, aggressive, incapable of relaxation in taking the smallest issues too seriously; and are somewhat disliked for the way that they're always rushing and demanding other people to serve to their standards of satisfaction.

a. 28-hour day
b. 33 Strategies of War
c. 1990 Clean Air Act
d. Type A and Type B personality theory

Chapter 10. Communicating and Information Technology

1. A _____ is a commercial building for storage of goods. _____s are used by manufacturers, importers, exporters, wholesalers, transport businesses, customs, etc. They are usually large plain buildings in industrial areas of cities and towns.

    a. 1990 Clean Air Act
    b. 28-hour day
    c. 33 Strategies of War
    d. Warehouse

2. _____ is a subfield of the larger discipline of communication studies. _____, as a field, is the consideration, analysis, and criticism of the role of communication in organizational contexts.

    The field traces its lineage through business information, business communication, and early mass communication studies published in the 1930s through the 1950s.

    a. A Stake in the Outcome
    b. A4e
    c. AAAI
    d. Organizational communication

3. _____ describes the situation when output from (or information about the result of) an event or phenomenon in the past will influence the same event/phenomenon in the present or future. When an event is part of a chain of cause-and-effect that forms a circuit or loop, then the event is said to 'feed back' into itself.

    _____ is also a synonym for:

    - _____ signal; the information about the initial event that is the basis for subsequent modification of the event.
    - _____ loop; the causal path that leads from the initial generation of the _____ signal to the subsequent modification of the event.

    _____ is a mechanism, process or signal that is looped back to control a system within itself. Such a loop is called a _____ loop.

    a. 1990 Clean Air Act
    b. Feedback loop
    c. Positive feedback
    d. Feedback

4. _____ is a form of communication that typically attempts to persuade potential customers to purchase or to consume more of a particular brand of product or service. 'While now central to the contemporary global economy and the reproduction of global production networks, it is only quite recently that _____ has been more than a marginal influence on patterns of sales and production. The formation of modern _____ was intimately bound up with the emergence of new forms of monopoly capitalism around the end of the 19th and beginning of the 20th century as one element in corporate strategies to create, organize and where possible control markets, especially for mass produced consumer goods.
   a. AAAI
   b. A4e
   c. A Stake in the Outcome
   d. Advertising

5. _____ , often measured as an _____ Quotient (EQ), is a term that describes the ability, capacity, skill or (in the case of the trait _____ model) a self-perceived ability, to identify, assess, and manage the emotions of one's self, of others, and of groups. Different models have been proposed for the definition of _____ and disagreement exists as to how the term should be used. Despite these disagreements, which are often highly technical, the ability _____ and trait _____ models (but not the mixed models) are enjoying considerable support in the literature and have successful applications in many different domains.
   a. A4e
   b. AAAI
   c. A Stake in the Outcome
   d. Emotional intelligence

6. The _____ captures an expanded spectrum of values and criteria for measuring organizational success: economic, ecological and social. With the ratification of the United Nations and ICLEI _____ standard for urban and community accounting in early 2007, this became the dominant approach to public sector full cost accounting. Similar UN standards apply to natural capital and human capital measurement to assist in measurements required by _____, e.g. the ecoBudget standard for reporting ecological footprint.
   a. 28-hour day
   b. 1990 Clean Air Act
   c. Triple bottom line
   d. 33 Strategies of War

7. _____ constitute a class of computer-based information systems including knowledge-based systems that support decision-making activities.

_____ are a specific class of computerized information systems that supports business and organizational decision-making activities. A properly-designed _____ is an interactive software-based system intended to help decision makers compile useful information from raw data, documents, personal knowledge, and/or business models to identify and solve problems and make decisions.

Chapter 10. Communicating and Information Technology   93

   a. 1990 Clean Air Act
   b. 28-hour day
   c. Decision support systems
   d. Spatial Decision Support Systems

8. An _____ is a type of management information system intended to facilitate and support the information and decision-making needs of senior executives by providing easy access to both internal and external information relevant to meeting the strategic goals of the organization. It is commonly considered as a specialized form of a Decision Support System (DSS)

The emphasis of _____ is on graphical displays and easy-to-use user interfaces. They offer strong reporting and drill-down capabilities.

   a. AAAI
   b. A4e
   c. A Stake in the Outcome
   d. Executive information system

9. An _____ is software that attempts to reproduce the performance of one or more human experts, most commonly in a specific problem domain, and is a traditional application and/or subfield of artificial intelligence. A wide variety of methods can be used to simulate the performance of the expert however common to most or all are 1) the creation of a so-called 'knowledgebase' which uses some knowledge representation formalism to capture the Subject Matter Experts (SME) knowledge and 2) a process of gathering that knowledge from the SME and codifying it according to the formalism, which is called knowledge engineering. _____s may or may not have learning components but a third common element is that once the system is developed it is proven by being placed in the same real world problem solving situation as the human SME, typically as an aid to human workers or a supplement to some information system.
   a. Expert system
   b. AAAI
   c. A Stake in the Outcome
   d. A4e

10. A _____ is a subset of the overall internal controls of a business covering the application of people, documents, technologies, and procedures by management accountants to solving business problems such as costing a product, service or a business-wide strategy. _____s are distinct from regular information systems in that they are used to analyze other information systems applied in operational activities in the organization. Academically, the term is commonly used to refer to the group of information management methods tied to the automation or support of human decision making, e.g. Decision Support Systems, Expert systems, and Executive information systems.

a. Management information system
b. Strategic information system
c. 1990 Clean Air Act
d. 28-hour day

11. An _____ is a private computer network that uses Internet technologies to securely share any part of an organization's information or operational systems with its employees. Sometimes the term refers only to the organization's internal website, but often it is a more extensive part of the organization's computer infrastructure and private websites are an important component and focal point of internal communication and collaboration.

An _____ is built from the same concepts and technologies used for the Internet, such as client-server computing and the Internet Protocol Suite (TCP/IP.)

a. A4e
b. Intranet
c. A Stake in the Outcome
d. AAAI

12. _____, commonly referred to as 'eBusiness' or 'e-Business', may be defined as the utilization of information and communication technologies (ICT) in support of all the activities of business. Commerce constitutes the exchange of products and services between businesses, groups and individuals and hence can be seen as one of the essential activities of any business. Hence, electronic commerce or eCommerce focuses on the use of ICT to enable the external activities and relationships of the business with individuals, groups and other businesses.
a. A Stake in the Outcome
b. A4e
c. Electronic business
d. AAAI

13. _____, commonly known as e-commerce, consists of the buying and selling of products or services over electronic systems such as the Internet and other computer networks. The amount of trade conducted electronically has grown extraordinarily with widespread Internet usage. The use of commerce is conducted in this way, spurring and drawing on innovations in electronic funds transfer, supply chain management, Internet marketing, online transaction processing, electronic data interchange (EDI), inventory management systems, and automated data collection systems.
a. A Stake in the Outcome
b. A4e
c. Electronic Commerce
d. Online shopping

Chapter 10. Communicating and Information Technology 95

14. _____ describes commerce transactions between businesses, such as between a manufacturer and a wholesaler, or between a wholesaler and a retailer. Contrasting terms are business-to-consumer (B2C) and business-to-government (B2G.)

The volume of B2B transactions is much higher than the volume of B2C transactions.

   a. Product bundling
   b. Market environment
   c. Category management
   d. Business-to-business

15. Business-to-consumer describes activities of businesses serving end consumers with products and/or services.

An example of a _____ transaction would be a person buying a pair of shoes from a retailer. The transactions that led to the shoes being available for purchase, that is the purchase of the leather, laces, rubber, etc.

   a. PEST analysis
   b. B2C
   c. Green marketing
   d. Market environment

16. _____ refers to the structured transmission of data between organizations by electronic means. It is used to transfer electronic documents from one computer system to another (ie) from one trading partner to another trading partner. It is more than mere E-mail; for instance, organizations might replace bills of lading and even checks with appropriate _____ messages.
   a. Electronic data interchange
   b. A Stake in the Outcome
   c. AAAI
   d. A4e

17. _____ is an advertisement in which a particular product specifically mentions a competitor by name for the express purpose of showing why the competitor is inferior to the product naming it.

This should not be confused with parody advertisements, where a fictional product is being advertised for the purpose of poking fun at the particular advertisement, nor should it be confused with the use of a coined brand name for the purpose of comparing the product without actually naming an actual competitor. ('Wikipedia tastes better and is less filling than the Encyclopedia Galactica.')

In the 1980s, during what has been referred to as the cola wars, soft-drink manufacturer Pepsi ran a series of advertisements where people, caught on hidden camera, in a blind taste test, chose Pepsi over rival Coca-Cola.

a. 28-hour day
b. 33 Strategies of War
c. Comparative advertising
d. 1990 Clean Air Act

18. A _____ is one of several ways of doing research whether it is social science related or even socially related. It is an intensive study of a single group, incident, or community. Other ways include experiments, surveys, multiple histories, and analysis of archival information.

Rather than using samples and following a rigid protocol to examine limited number of variables, _____ methods involve an in-depth, longitudinal examination of a single instance or event: a case.

a. Standard operating procedure
b. 1990 Clean Air Act
c. Longitudinal study
d. Case study

19. In probability theory, the _____ of any event A is the event [not A], i.e. the event that A does not occur. The event A and its _____ [not A] are mutually exclusive and exhaustive. Generally, there is only one event B such that A and B are both mutually exclusive and exhaustive; that event is the _____ of A. The _____ of an event A is sometimes denoted A'.

a. Strict liability
b. Distribution
c. Probability-generating function
d. Complement

Chapter 11. Motivating for High Performance

1. A _____ is a prediction that directly or indirectly causes itself to become true, by the very terms of the prophecy itself, due to positive feedback between belief and behavior. Although examples of such prophecies can be found in literature as far back as ancient Greece and ancient India, it is 20th-century sociologist Robert K. Merton who is credited with coining the expression '_____' and formalizing its structure and consequences. In his book Social Theory and Social Structure, Merton gives as a feature of the _____:

In other words, a prophecy declared as truth when it is actually false may sufficiently influence people, either through fear or logical confusion, so that their reactions ultimately fulfill the once-false prophecy.

   a. 1990 Clean Air Act
   b. 28-hour day
   c. 33 Strategies of War
   d. Self-fulfilling prophecy

2. In operant conditioning, _____ occurs when an event following a response causes an increase in the probability of that response occurring in the future. Response strength can be assessed by measures such as the frequency with which the response is made (for example, a pigeon may peck a key more times in the session), or the speed with which it is made (for example, a rat may run a maze faster.) The environment change contingent upon the response is called a reinforcer.
   a. Meetings, Incentives, Conferences, and Exhibitions
   b. Diminishing Manufacturing Sources and Material Shortages
   c. Historiometry
   d. Reinforcement

3. Clayton Paul Alderfer is an American psychologist who further expanded Maslow's hierarchy of needs by categorizing the hierarchy into his _____ Alderfer categorized the lower order needs (Physiological and Safety) into the Existence category. He fit Maslow's interpersonal love and esteem needs into the relatedness category. The growth category contained the Self Actualization and self esteem needs.

Alderfer also proposed a regression theory to go along with the _____. He said that when needs in a higher category are not met then individuals redouble the efforts invested in a lower category need.

   a. Adam Smith
   b. Alvin Neill Jackson
   c. Abraham Harold Maslow
   d. ERG theory

4. _____ is a term that has been used in various psychology theories, often in slightly different ways (e.g., Goldstein, Maslow, Rogers.) The term was originally introduced by the organismic theorist Kurt Goldstein for the motive to realise all of one's potentialities. In his view, it is the master motive--indeed, the only real motive a person has, all others being merely manifestations of it.

a. 33 Strategies of War
b. 1990 Clean Air Act
c. Self-actualization
d. 28-hour day

5. _____ was developed by Frederick Herzberg, a psychologist who found that job satisfaction and job dissatisfaction acted independently of each other. _____ states that there are certain factors in the workplace that cause job satisfaction, while a separate set of factors cause dissatisfaction.

a. Need for power
b. 1990 Clean Air Act
c. Need for Achievement
d. Two-factor theory

6. Maslow's _____ is a theory in psychology, proposed by Abraham Maslow in his 1943 paper A Theory of Human Motivation, which he subsequently extended to include his observations of humans' innate curiosity.

Maslow's _____ is predetermined in order of importance. It is often depicted as a pyramid consisting of five levels: the lowest level is associated with physiological needs, while the uppermost level is associated with self-actualization needs, particularly those related to identity and purpose. Deficiency needs must be met first. Once these are met, seeking to satisfy growth needs drives personal growth. The higher needs in this hierarchy only come into focus when the lower needs in the pyramid are met.

a. 28-hour day
b. 1990 Clean Air Act
c. Hierarchy of needs
d. 33 Strategies of War

7. _____ is a term that was popularized by renowned psychologist David McClelland in 1961. However, it should be recognized that McClellend's thinking was strongly influenced by the pioneering work of Henry Murray who first identified underlying psychological human needs and motivational processes (1938.) It was Murray who set out a taxonomy of needs, including Achievement, Power and Affiliation - and placed these in the context of an integrated motivational model.

a. 1990 Clean Air Act
b. Need for Achievement
c. Two-factor theory
d. Need for power

8. _____ refers to an individual's desire for significant accomplishment, mastering of skills, control, or high standards. The term was introduced by the psychologist, David McClelland.

_____ is related to the difficulty of tasks people choose to undertake.

a. 1990 Clean Air Act
b. Need for power
c. Two-factor theory
d. Need for achievement

9. _____ attempts to explain relational satisfaction in terms of perceptions of fair/unfair distributions of resources within interpersonal relationships. _____ is considered as one of the justice theories, It was first developed in 1962 by John Stacey Adams, a workplace and behavioral psychologist, who asserted that employees seek to maintain equity between the inputs that they bring to a job and the outcomes that they receive from it against the perceived inputs and outcomes of others (Adams, 1965.) The belief is that people value fair treatment which causes them to be motivated to keep the fairness maintained within the relationships of their co-workers and the organization.

a. AAAI
b. A Stake in the Outcome
c. Equity theory
d. A4e

10. _____ is about the mental processes regarding choice, or choosing. It explains the processes that an individual undergoes to make choices. In organizational behavior study, _____ is a motivation theory first proposed by Victor Vroom of the Yale School of Management.

a. Expectancy theory
b. AAAI
c. A Stake in the Outcome
d. A4e

11. _____ has become one of the most popular theories in organizational psychology.

Goal setting has been a formula used for acheivement since the early 1800s. The form and pattern has cahanged drastically over the years and there is still much debate as to what is the most efective pattern to follow.

a. Human relations
b. Job satisfaction
c. Goal-setting theory
d. Corporate Culture

Chapter 11. Motivating for High Performance

12. A _____ is a framework for creating economic, social, and/or other forms of value. The term _____ is thus used for a broad range of informal and formal descriptions to represent core aspects of a business, including purpose, offerings, strategies, infrastructure, organizational structures, trading practices, and operational processes and policies.

Conceptualizations of _____s try to formalize informal descriptions into building blocks and their relationships.

   a. Gap analysis
   b. Business model
   c. Business model design
   d. Business networking

13. _____ involves establishing specific, measurable and time-targeted objectives. Work on the theory of goal-setting suggests that it's an effective tool for making progress by ensuring that participants in a group with a common goal are clearly aware of what is expected from them if an objective is to be achieved. On a personal level, setting goals is a process that allows people to specify then work towards their own objectives - most commonly with financial or career-based goals.

   a. Resource-based view
   b. Catfish effect
   c. Digital strategy
   d. Goal setting

14. In probability theory, a probability distribution is called _____ if its cumulative distribution function is _____. This is equivalent to saying that for random variables X with the distribution in question, Pr[X = a] = 0 for all real numbers a, i.e.: the probability that X attains the value a is zero, for any number a. If the distribution of X is _____ then X is called a _____ random variable.

   a. Continuous
   b. Connectionist expert systems
   c. Decision tree pruning
   d. Pay Band

15. When an animal's surroundings are controlled, its behavior patterns after reinforcement become predictable, even for very complex behavior patterns. A schedule of reinforcement is the protocol for determining when responses or behaviors will be reinforced, ranging from _____, in which every response is reinforced, and extinction, in which no response is reinforced. Between these extremes is intermittent or partial reinforcement where only some responses are reinforced.

   a. Recognition-primed decision
   b. Clinical decision support systems
   c. Pension System
   d. Continuous reinforcement

16. _____ is one of the four Ps of the marketing mix. The other three aspects are product, promotion, and place. It is also a key variable in microeconomic price allocation theory.
   a. Penetration pricing
   b. Price floor
   c. Transfer pricing
   d. Pricing

17. A _____ is one of several ways of doing research whether it is social science related or even socially related. It is an intensive study of a single group, incident, or community.Other ways include experiments, surveys, multiple histories, and analysis of archival information .

Rather than using samples and following a rigid protocol to examine limited number of variables, _____ methods involve an in-depth, longitudinal examination of a single instance or event: a case.

   a. 1990 Clean Air Act
   b. Longitudinal study
   c. Standard operating procedure
   d. Case study

Chapter 12. Team Leadership

1. The _____ or gross domestic income (GDI), a basic measure of an economy's economic performance, is the market value of all final goods and services made within the borders of a nation in a year. _____ can be defined in three ways, all of which are conceptually identical. First, it is equal to the total expenditures for all final goods and services produced within the country in a stipulated period of time (usually a 365-day year).
    a. Human capital
    b. Productivity management
    c. Perfect competition
    d. Gross domestic product

2. In mathematics, a _____ law is (roughly speaking) a formal power series behaving as if it were the product of a Lie group. They were first defined in 1946 by S. Bochner. The term _____ sometimes means the same as _____ law, and sometimes means one of several generalizations.
    a. Formal group
    b. 28-hour day
    c. 1990 Clean Air Act
    d. 33 Strategies of War

3. In sociology and anthropology, an action group or _____ is a group of people joined temporarily to accomplish some task or take part in some organized collective action.

As an example, imagine that in a hypothetical culture, four bridesmaids are traditionally selected to play a role in a wedding ceremony, and eligibility to be chosen as a bridesmaid is dependent on being a young, female relative of the bride. Several people may fall into this social category: they have no automatic entitlement to the role but are eligible to assume it if chosen.

    a. 1990 Clean Air Act
    b. 28-hour day
    c. 33 Strategies of War
    d. Task group

4. A _____ -- also known as a geographically dispersed team -- is a group of individuals who work across time, space, and organizational boundaries with links strengthened by webs of communication technology. They have complementary skills and are committed to a common purpose, have interdependent performance goals, and share an approach to work for which they hold themselves mutually accountable. Geographically dispersed teams allow organizations to hire and retain the best people regardless of location.
    a. Risk management
    b. Virtual team
    c. Trademark
    d. Kanban

5. _____ is a term used in the stock-trading world to describe the practice of buying shares or other securities without actually having the capital to cover the trade. This is possible when recently bought or sold shares are unsettled, and therefore have not been paid for.

Since stock transactions usually settle after three business days, a crafty trader can buy a stock and sell it the following day, without ever having sufficient funds in the account.

   a. Free riding
   b. 1990 Clean Air Act
   c. Shareholder
   d. Stockholder

6. _____ has been described as the 'process of social influence in which one person can enlist the aid and support of others in the accomplishment of a common task' . A definition more inclusive of followers comes from Alan Keith of Genentech who said '_____ is ultimately about creating a way for people to contribute to making something extraordinary happen.'

_____ is one of the most salient aspects of the organizational context. However, defining _____ has been challenging.

   a. 28-hour day
   b. Situational leadership
   c. 1990 Clean Air Act
   d. Leadership

7. An _____ is a mostly hierarchical concept of subordination of entities that collaborate and contribute to serve one common aim.

Organizations are a variant of clustered entities. The structure of an organization is usually set up in many a styles, dependent on their objectives and ambience.

   a. Organizational development
   b. Informal organization
   c. Open shop
   d. Organizational structure

8. _____ is the study of groups, and also a general term for group processes. Relevant to the fields of psychology, sociology, and communication studies, a group is two or more individuals who are connected to each other by social relationships. Because they interact and influence each other, groups develop a number of dynamic processes that separate them from a random collection of individuals.

a. 1990 Clean Air Act
b. Collective action
c. 28-hour day
d. Group dynamics

9. _____ can be regarded as an outcome of mental processes (cognitive process) leading to the selection of a course of action among several alternatives. Every _____ process produces a final choice. The output can be an action or an opinion of choice.
   a. Decision making
   b. 28-hour day
   c. 33 Strategies of War
   d. 1990 Clean Air Act

10. _____ is a range of processes aimed at alleviating or eliminating sources of conflict. The term '_____' is sometimes used interchangeably with the term dispute resolution or alternative dispute resolution. Processes of _____ generally include negotiation, mediation and diplomacy.
    a. 33 Strategies of War
    b. 28-hour day
    c. 1990 Clean Air Act
    d. Conflict resolution

11. The goal of most research on _____ is to learn why and how small groups change over time. To do this, researchers examine patterns of change and continuity in groups over time. Aspects of a group that might be studied include the quality of the output produced by a group, the type and frequency of its activities, its cohesiveness, the existence of conflict, etc.
    a. Group development
    b. 28-hour day
    c. 33 Strategies of War
    d. 1990 Clean Air Act

12. A _____ is a list of the general tasks and responsibilities of a position. Typically, it also includes to whom the position reports, specifications such as the qualifications needed by the person in the job, salary range for the position, etc. A _____ is usually developed by conducting a job analysis, which includes examining the tasks and sequences of tasks necessary to perform the job.

a. Recruitment Process Insourcing
b. Recruitment advertising
c. Recruitment
d. Job description

13. _____ is a civil designation for persons who are incorporated in a fixed or permanent way to a society or group: regular member of the working staff, permanent staff distinguished from a supernumerary.

The term '_____' and its counterpart, 'supernumerary,' originated in Spanish and Latin American academy and government; it is now also used in countries all over the world, such as France, the U.S., England, Italy, etc.

There are _____ members of surgical organizations, of universities, of gastronomical associations, etc.

a. Affiliation
b. Adam Smith
c. Abraham Harold Maslow
d. Numerary

14. A _____ is one of several ways of doing research whether it is social science related or even socially related. It is an intensive study of a single group, incident, or community.Other ways include experiments, surveys, multiple histories, and analysis of archival information .

Rather than using samples and following a rigid protocol to examine limited number of variables, _____ methods involve an in-depth, longitudinal examination of a single instance or event: a case.

a. 1990 Clean Air Act
b. Longitudinal study
c. Standard operating procedure
d. Case study

Chapter 13. Control Systems: Financial and Human

1. _____ is one of the managerial functions like planning, organizing, staffing and directing. It is an important function because it helps to check the errors and to take the corrective action so that deviation from standards are minimized and stated goals of the organization are achieved in desired manner. According to modern concepts, _____ is a foreseeing action whereas earlier concept of _____ was used only when errors were detected. _____ in management means setting standards, measuring actual performance and taking corrective action.

   a. Control
   b. Decision tree pruning
   c. Turnover
   d. Schedule of reinforcement

2. _____ describes the situation when output from (or information about the result of) an event or phenomenon in the past will influence the same event/phenomenon in the present or future. When an event is part of a chain of cause-and-effect that forms a circuit or loop, then the event is said to 'feed back' into itself.

   _____ is also a synonym for:

   - _____ signal; the information about the initial event that is the basis for subsequent modification of the event.
   - _____ loop; the causal path that leads from the initial generation of the _____ signal to the subsequent modification of the event.

   _____ is a mechanism, process or signal that is looped back to control a system within itself. Such a loop is called a _____ loop.

   a. Positive feedback
   b. Feedback
   c. 1990 Clean Air Act
   d. Feedback loop

3. _____ is an advertisement in which a particular product specifically mentions a competitor by name for the express purpose of showing why the competitor is inferior to the product naming it.

This should not be confused with parody advertisements, where a fictional product is being advertised for the purpose of poking fun at the particular advertisement, nor should it be confused with the use of a coined brand name for the purpose of comparing the product without actually naming an actual competitor. ('Wikipedia tastes better and is less filling than the Encyclopedia Galactica.')

In the 1980s, during what has been referred to as the cola wars, soft-drink manufacturer Pepsi ran a series of advertisements where people, caught on hidden camera, in a blind taste test, chose Pepsi over rival Coca-Cola.

a. 1990 Clean Air Act
b. Comparative advertising
c. 33 Strategies of War
d. 28-hour day

4. In economics, business, retail, and accounting, a _____ is the value of money that has been used up to produce something, and hence is not available for use anymore. In economics, a _____ is an alternative that is given up as a result of a decision. In business, the _____ may be one of acquisition, in which case the amount of money expended to acquire it is counted as _____.
   a. Cost allocation
   b. Cost
   c. Cost overrun
   d. Fixed costs

5. _____ is a business Advocate term for an element which is necessary for an organization or project to achieve its mission. They are the critical factors or activities required for ensuring the success of your business. The term was initially used in the world of data analysis, and business analysis.
   a. Business hours
   b. Customer satisfaction
   c. Critical success factor
   d. Collaborative leadership

6. The general definition of an _____ is an evaluation of a person, organization, system, process, project or product. _____s are performed to ascertain the validity and reliability of information; also to provide an assessment of a system's internal control. The goal of an _____ is to express an opinion on the person / organization/system (etc) in question, under evaluation based on work done on a test basis.
   a. Audit committee
   b. A Stake in the Outcome
   c. Internal control
   d. Audit

7. _____ is a profession and activity involved in helping organisations achieve their stated objectives. It does this by using a systematic methodology for analyzing business processes, procedures and activities with the goal of highlighting organizational problems and recommending solutions. Professionals called internal auditors are employed by organizations to perform the _____ activity.

Chapter 13. Control Systems: Financial and Human

a. Audit committee
b. Internal control
c. A Stake in the Outcome
d. Internal auditing

8. A _____ is a type of bar chart that illustrates a project schedule. _____s illustrate the start and finish dates of the terminal elements and summary elements of a project. Terminal elements and summary elements comprise the work breakdown structure of the project.

   a. 33 Strategies of War
   b. 1990 Clean Air Act
   c. 28-hour day
   d. Gantt chart

9. The Program (or Project) Evaluation and Review Technique, commonly abbreviated _____, is a model for project management designed to analyze and represent the tasks involved in completing a given project.

_____ is a method to analyze the involved tasks in completing a given project, specially the time needed to complete each task, and identifying the minimum time needed to complete the total project.

_____ was developed primarily to simplify the planning and scheduling of large and complex projects.

   a. 28-hour day
   b. 33 Strategies of War
   c. 1990 Clean Air Act
   d. PERT

10. _____ refers to the movement of cash into or out of a business or financial product. It is usually measured during a specified, finite period of time. Measurement of _____ can be used

   - to determine a project's rate of return or value. The time of _____s into and out of projects are used as inputs in financial models such as internal rate of return, and net present value.
   - to determine problems with a business's liquidity. Being profitable does not necessarily mean being liquid. A company can fail because of a shortage of cash, even while profitable.
   - as an alternate measure of a business's profits when it is believed that accrual accounting concepts do not represent economic realities. For example, a company may be notionally profitable but generating little operational cash (as may be the case for a company that barters its products rather than selling for cash.) In such a case, the company may be deriving additional operating cash by issuing shares evaluating default risk, re-investment requirements, etc.

_____ is a generic term used differently depending on the context. It may be defined by users for their own purposes.

a. Gross profit
b. Gross profit margin
c. Sweat equity
d. Cash flow

11. _____ are formal records of the financial activities of a business, person, or other entity. In British English, including United Kingdom company law, _____ are often referred to as accounts, although the term _____ is also used, particularly by accountants.

_____ provide an overview of a business or person's financial condition in both short and long term.

a. 1990 Clean Air Act
b. Financial statements
c. 28-hour day
d. 33 Strategies of War

12. _____s (CAPEX or capex) are expenditures creating future benefits. A _____ is incurred when a business spends money either to buy fixed assets or to add to the value of an existing fixed asset with a useful life that extends beyond the taxable year. Capex are used by a company to acquire or upgrade physical assets such as equipment, property, or industrial buildings.
a. Weighted average cost of capital
b. 1990 Clean Air Act
c. Capital expenditure
d. Capital intensive

13. _____ generally refers to a list of all planned expenses and revenues. It is a plan for saving and spending. A _____ is an important concept in microeconomics, which uses a _____ line to illustrate the trade-offs between two or more goods.
a. 28-hour day
b. 33 Strategies of War
c. Budget
d. 1990 Clean Air Act

14. _____ is the planning process used to determine whether a firm's long term investments such as new machinery, replacement machinery, new plants, new products, and research development projects are worth pursuing. It is budget for major capital, or investment, expenditures.

Many formal methods are used in _____, including the techniques such as

- Net present value
- Profitability index
- Internal rate of return
- Modified Internal Rate of Return
- Equivalent annuity

These methods use the incremental cash flows from each potential investment, or project. Techniques based on accounting earnings and accounting rules are sometimes used - though economists consider this to be improper - such as the accounting rate of return, and 'return on investment.' Simplified and hybrid methods are used as well, such as payback period and discounted payback period.

a. Gross profit margin
b. Capital budgeting
c. Restricted stock
d. Gross profit

15. In financial accounting, a _____ or statement of financial position is a summary of a person's or organization's balances. Assets, liabilities and ownership equity are listed as of a specific date, such as the end of its financial year. A _____ is often described as a snapshot of a company's financial condition.

a. 33 Strategies of War
b. 1990 Clean Air Act
c. Balance sheet
d. 28-hour day

16. _____ is a company's financial statement that indicates how the revenue is transformed into the net income The purpose of the _____ is to show managers and investors whether the company made or lost money during the period being reported.

The important thing to remember about an _____ is that it represents a period of time.

a. AAAI
b. A Stake in the Outcome
c. A4e
d. Income statement

17. _____, sometimes referred to as 'cumulative causation', is a feedback loop system in which the system responds to perturbation in the same direction as the perturbation. In contrast, a system that responds to the perturbation in the opposite direction is called a negative feedback system. These concepts were first recognized as broadly applicable by Norbert Wiener in his 1948 work on cybernetics.
   a. Feedback loop
   b. Negative feedback
   c. 1990 Clean Air Act
   d. Positive feedback

18. _____ is unwelcome harassment of a sexual nature, or based upon the receiving party's sex or gender. In some contexts or circumstances, _____ may be illegal. It includes a range of behavior from seemingly mild transgressions and annoyances to actual sexual abuse or sexual assault.
   a. Hypernorms
   b. Sexual harassment
   c. 28-hour day
   d. 1990 Clean Air Act

19. A _____ is one of several ways of doing research whether it is social science related or even socially related. It is an intensive study of a single group, incident, or community.Other ways include experiments, surveys, multiple histories, and analysis of archival information .

Rather than using samples and following a rigid protocol to examine limited number of variables, _____ methods involve an in-depth, longitudinal examination of a single instance or event: a case.

   a. Standard operating procedure
   b. Longitudinal study
   c. Case study
   d. 1990 Clean Air Act

Chapter 14. Operations, Quality, and Productivity

1. In economics, business, retail, and accounting, a _____ is the value of money that has been used up to produce something, and hence is not available for use anymore. In economics, a _____ is an alternative that is given up as a result of a decision. In business, the _____ may be one of acquisition, in which case the amount of money expended to acquire it is counted as _____.
    a. Cost overrun
    b. Cost allocation
    c. Fixed costs
    d. Cost

2. _____ is the process whereby companies use cost accounting to report or control the various costs of doing business.

   _____ generally describes the approaches and activities of managers in short run and long run planning and control decisions that increase value for customers and lower costs of products and services.

    a. Genbutsu
    b. Missing completely at random
    c. Strict liability
    d. Cost Management

3. Levi Strauss, born Löb Strauss (February 26, 1829 - September 26, 1902) was a German-Jewish immigrant to the United States who founded the first company to manufacture blue jeans. His firm, _____, began in 1853 in San Francisco, California.

   Levi Strauss was born in Bavaria, Germany, to Hirsch Strauss and his wife Rebecca (Haas) Strauss.

    a. Abraham Harold Maslow
    b. Adam Smith
    c. Affiliation
    d. Levi Strauss ' Company

4. _____ is one of the managerial functions like planning, organizing, staffing and directing. It is an important function because it helps to check the errors and to take the corrective action so that deviation from standards are minimized and stated goals of the organization are achieved in desired manner. According to modern concepts, _____ is a foreseeing action whereas earlier concept of _____ was used only when errors were detected. _____ in management means setting standards, measuring actual performance and taking corrective action.

Chapter 14. Operations, Quality, and Productivity

a. Decision tree pruning
b. Turnover
c. Schedule of reinforcement
d. Control

5. _____ refers to the movement of cash into or out of a business or financial product. It is usually measured during a specified, finite period of time. Measurement of _____ can be used

- to determine a project's rate of return or value. The time of _____s into and out of projects are used as inputs in financial models such as internal rate of return, and net present value.
- to determine problems with a business's liquidity. Being profitable does not necessarily mean being liquid. A company can fail because of a shortage of cash, even while profitable.
- as an alternate measure of a business's profits when it is believed that accrual accounting concepts do not represent economic realities. For example, a company may be notionally profitable but generating little operational cash (as may be the case for a company that barters its products rather than selling for cash.) In such a case, the company may be deriving additional operating cash by issuing shares evaluating default risk, re-investment requirements, etc.

_____ is a generic term used differently depending on the context. It may be defined by users for their own purposes.

a. Gross profit
b. Gross profit margin
c. Sweat equity
d. Cash flow

6. _____ is the use of control systems (such as numerical control, programmable logic control, and other industrial control systems), in concert with other applications of information technology (such as computer-aided technologies [CAD, CAM, CAx]), to control industrial machinery and processes, reducing the need for human intervention. In the scope of industrialization, _____ is a step beyond mechanization. Whereas mechanization provided human operators with machinery to assist them with the physical requirements of work, _____ greatly reduces the need for human sensory and mental requirements as well.

a. A Stake in the Outcome
b. A4e
c. AAAI
d. Automation

7. _____ in engineering is a method of manufacturing in which the entire production process is controlled by computer. The traditional separated process methods are joined through a computer by CIM. This integration allows that the processes exchange information with each other and they are able to initiate actions.

a. 28-hour day
b. 33 Strategies of War
c. Computer-integrated manufacturing
d. 1990 Clean Air Act

8. _____ is an advertisement in which a particular product specifically mentions a competitor by name for the express purpose of showing why the competitor is inferior to the product naming it.

This should not be confused with parody advertisements, where a fictional product is being advertised for the purpose of poking fun at the particular advertisement, nor should it be confused with the use of a coined brand name for the purpose of comparing the product without actually naming an actual competitor. ('Wikipedia tastes better and is less filling than the Encyclopedia Galactica.')

In the 1980s, during what has been referred to as the cola wars, soft-drink manufacturer Pepsi ran a series of advertisements where people, caught on hidden camera, in a blind taste test, chose Pepsi over rival Coca-Cola.

a. Comparative advertising
b. 28-hour day
c. 1990 Clean Air Act
d. 33 Strategies of War

9. A _____ system is a manufacturing system in which there is some amount of flexibility that allows the system to react in the case of changes, whether predicted or unpredicted. This flexibility is generally considered to fall into two categories, which both contain numerous subcategories.

The first category, machine flexibility, covers the system's ability to be changed to produce new product types, and ability to change the order of operations executed on a part. The second category is called routing flexibility, which consists of the ability to use multiple machines to perform the same operation on a part, as well as the system's ability to absorb large-scale changes, such as in volume, capacity, or capability.

a. Manufacturing resource planning
b. Jidoka
c. Flexible manufacturing
d. Homeworkers

10. _____ is an increasingly broadening term with which an organization, or other human system describes the combination of traditionally administrative personnel functions with acquisition and application of skills, knowledge and experience, Employee Relations and resource planning at various levels. The field draws upon concepts developed in Industrial/Organizational Psychology and System Theory. _____ has at least two related interpretations depending on context. The original usage derives from political economy and economics, where it was traditionally called labor, one of four factors of production although this perspective is changing as a function of new and ongoing research into more strategic approaches at national levels. This first usage is used more in terms of '_____ development', and can go beyond just organizations to the level of nations. The more traditional usage within corporations and businesses refers to the individuals within a firm or agency, and to the portion of the organization that deals with hiring, firing, training, and other personnel issues, typically referred to as `_____ management'.

 a. Bradford Factor
 b. Progressive discipline
 c. Human resources
 d. Human resource management

11. _____ is the process of determining the production capacity needed by an organization to meet changing demands for its products. In the context of _____, 'capacity' is the maximum amount of work that an organization is capable of completing in a given period of time.

A discrepancy between the capacity of an organization and the demands of its customers results in inefficiency, either in under-utilized resources or unfulfilled customers.

 a. Scientific management
 b. Productivity
 c. Capacity planning
 d. Remanufacturing

12. The Program (or Project) Evaluation and Review Technique, commonly abbreviated _____, is a model for project management designed to analyze and represent the tasks involved in completing a given project.

_____ is a method to analyze the involved tasks in completing a given project, specially the time needed to complete each task, and identifying the minimum time needed to complete the total project.

_____ was developed primarily to simplify the planning and scheduling of large and complex projects.

 a. 33 Strategies of War
 b. 1990 Clean Air Act
 c. PERT
 d. 28-hour day

Chapter 14. Operations, Quality, and Productivity

13. A _____ is a type of bar chart that illustrates a project schedule. _____s illustrate the start and finish dates of the terminal elements and summary elements of a project. Terminal elements and summary elements comprise the work breakdown structure of the project.

   a. 33 Strategies of War
   b. Gantt chart
   c. 1990 Clean Air Act
   d. 28-hour day

14. _____ are goods that have completed the manufacturing process but have not yet been sold or distributed to the end user.

Manufacturing has three classes of inventory:

1. Raw material
2. Work in process
3. _____

A good purchased as a 'raw material' goes into the manufacture of a product. A good only partially completed during the manufacturing process is called 'work in process'. When the good is completed as to manufacturing but not yet sold or distributed to the end-user is called a 'finished good'.

   a. Reorder point
   b. 28-hour day
   c. 1990 Clean Air Act
   d. Finished goods

15. _____ consists of the sale of goods or merchandise from a fixed location, such as a department store, boutique or kiosk in small or individual lots for direct consumption by the purchaser. _____ may include subordinated services, such as delivery. Purchasers may be individuals or businesses.

   a. 28-hour day
   b. 1990 Clean Air Act
   c. Planogram
   d. Retailing

16. _____ is the level of inventory that minimizes the total inventory holding costs and ordering costs. The framework used to determine this order quantity is also known as Wilson _____ Model. The model was developed by F. W. Harris in 1913.

a. Anti-leadership
b. Effective executive
c. Event management
d. Economic order quantity

17. _____ is a company-wide computer software system used to manage and coordinate all the resources, information, and functions of a business from shared data stores.

An _____ system has a service-oriented architecture with modular hardware and software units and 'services' that communicate on a local area network. The modular design allows a business to add or reconfigure modules (perhaps from different vendors) while preserving data integrity in one shared database that may be centralized or distributed.

a. AAAI
b. Enterprise resource planning
c. A Stake in the Outcome
d. A4e

18. _____ is an inventory strategy that strives to improve the return on investment of a business by reducing in-process inventory and its associated carrying costs. To meet _____ objectives, the process relies on signals between different points in the process. This means the process is often driven by a series of signals, or Kanban , which tell production when to make the next part. Kanban are usually 'tickets' but can be simple visual signals, such as the presence or absence of a part on a shelf. Implemented correctly, _____ can dramatically improve a manufacturing organization's return on investment, quality, and efficiency.
a. Just-in-time
b. 28-hour day
c. 33 Strategies of War
d. 1990 Clean Air Act

19. A _____ is the system of organizations, people, technology, activities, information and resources involved in moving a product or service from supplier to customer. _____ activities transform natural resources, raw materials and components into a finished product that is delivered to the end customer. In sophisticated _____ systems, used products may re-enter the _____ at any point where residual value is recyclable.
a. Drop shipping
b. Wholesalers
c. Packaging
d. Supply chain

Chapter 14. Operations, Quality, and Productivity

20. _____ is the use of an object (typically referred to as an RFID tag) applied to or incorporated into a product, animal, or person for the purpose of identification and tracking using radio waves. Some tags can be read from several meters away and beyond the line of sight of the reader.

Most RFID tags contain at least two parts.

   a. 1990 Clean Air Act
   b. Radio-frequency identification
   c. 33 Strategies of War
   d. 28-hour day

21. _____ refers to planned and systematic production processes that provide confidence in a product's suitability for its intended purpose. Refer to the definition by Merriam-Webster for further information . It is a set of activities intended to ensure that products (goods and/or services) satisfy customer requirements in a systematic, reliable fashion.
   a. Quality assurance
   b. Risk assessment
   c. 28-hour day
   d. 1990 Clean Air Act

22. In engineering and manufacturing, _____ and quality engineering are used in developing systems to ensure products or services are designed and produced to meet or exceed customer requirements. Refer to the definition by Merriam-Webster for further information . These systems are often developed in conjunction with other business and engineering disciplines using a cross-functional approach.
   a. Process capability
   b. Statistical process control
   c. Single Minute Exchange of Die
   d. Quality control

23. _____ is a business management strategy aimed at embedding awareness of quality in all organizational processes. _____ has been widely used in manufacturing, education, hospitals, call centers, government, and service industries, as well as NASA space and science programs.

As defined by the International Organization for Standardization (ISO):

> '_____ is a management approach for an organization, centered on quality, based on the participation of all its members and aiming at long-term success through customer satisfaction, and benefits to all members of the organization and to society.' ISO 8402:1994

One major aim is to reduce variation from every process so that greater consistency of effort is obtained. (Royse, D., Thyer, B., Padgett D., ' Logan T., 2006)

a. Total quality management
b. Quality management
c. 1990 Clean Air Act
d. 28-hour day

24. _____ refers to the process of grouping activities into departments.

Division of labour creates specialists who need coordination. This coordination is facilitated by grouping specialists together in departments.

a. Decent work
b. Maximum wage
c. Division of labour
d. Departmentalization

25. _____ is the management of a network of interconnected businesses involved in the ultimate provision of product and service packages required by end customers (Harland, 1996.) _____ spans all movement and storage of raw materials, work-in-process inventory, and finished goods from point of origin to point of consumption (supply chain.)

The definition an American professional association put forward is that _____ encompasses the planning and management of all activities involved in sourcing, procurement, conversion, and logistics management activities.

a. Freight forwarder
b. Supply chain management
c. Packaging
d. Drop shipping

26. _____ is a concept in ethics with several meanings. It is often used synonymously with such concepts as responsibility, answerability, enforcement, blameworthiness, liability and other terms associated with the expectation of account-giving. As an aspect of governance, it has been central to discussions related to problems in both the public and private (corporation) worlds.
a. A4e
b. Accountability
c. A Stake in the Outcome
d. Usury

Chapter 14. Operations, Quality, and Productivity

27. _____ is a family of standards for quality management systems. _____ is maintained by ISO, the International Organization for Standardization and is administered by accreditation and certification bodies. The rules are updated, the time and changes in the requirements for quality, motivate change.
    a. ISO 9000
    b. A4e
    c. A Stake in the Outcome
    d. AAAI

28. _____ is a business management strategy, initially implemented by Motorola, that today enjoys widespread application in many sectors of industry.

    _____ seeks to improve the quality of process outputs by identifying and removing the causes of defects (errors) and variation in manufacturing and business processes. It uses a set of quality management methods, including statistical methods, and creates a special infrastructure of people within the organization ('Black Belts' etc.)

    a. Theory of constraints
    b. Production line
    c. Six Sigma
    d. Takt time

29. _____ Movement refers to those researchers of organizational development who study the behavior of people in groups, in particular workplace groups. It originated in the 1920s' Hawthorne studies, which examined the effects of social relations, motivation and employee satisfaction on factory productivity. The movement viewed workers in terms of their psychology and fit with companies, rather than as interchangeable parts.
    a. Human relations
    b. Work design
    c. Participatory management
    d. Hersey-Blanchard situational theory

30. In statistics, _____ is:

    - the arithmetic _____
    - the expected value of a random variable, which is also called the population _____.

    It is sometimes stated that the '_____' _____s average. This is incorrect if '_____' is taken in the specific sense of 'arithmetic _____' as there are different types of averages: the _____, median, and mode. Other simple statistical analyses use measures of spread, such as range, interquartile range, or standard deviation. For a real-valued random variable X, the _____ is the expectation of X. Note that not every probability distribution has a defined _____; see the Cauchy distribution for an example.

a. Control chart
b. Statistical inference
c. Correlation
d. Mean

31. _____ is an effective method of monitoring a process through the use of control charts. Control charts enable the use of objective criteria for distinguishing background variation from events of significance based on statistical techniques. Much of its power lies in the ability to monitor both process center and its variation about that center.
a. Quality control
b. Process capability
c. Single Minute Exchange of Die
d. Statistical process control

32. The _____ states that, for many events, roughly 80% of the effects come from 20% of the causes. Business management thinker Joseph M. Juran suggested the principle and named it after Italian economist Vilfredo Pareto, who observed that 80% of the land in Italy was owned by 20% of the population. It is a common rule of thumb in business; e.g., '80% of your sales come from 20% of your clients.' Mathematically, where something is shared among a sufficiently large set of participants, there will always be a number k between 50 and 100 such that k% is taken by% of the participants.
a. Bylaw
b. Greenfield agreement
c. Board of directors
d. Pareto principle

33. _____ refers to metrics and measures of output from production processes, per unit of input. Labor _____, for example, is typically measured as a ratio of output per labor-hour, an input. _____ may be conceived of as a metrics of the technical or engineering efficiency of production.
a. Master production schedule
b. Value engineering
c. Remanufacturing
d. Productivity

34. _____ describes the situation when output from (or information about the result of) an event or phenomenon in the past will influence the same event/phenomenon in the present or future. When an event is part of a chain of cause-and-effect that forms a circuit or loop, then the event is said to 'feed back' into itself.

_____ is also a synonym for:

- _____ signal; the information about the initial event that is the basis for subsequent modification of the event.
- _____ loop; the causal path that leads from the initial generation of the _____ signal to the subsequent modification of the event.

_____ is a mechanism, process or signal that is looped back to control a system within itself. Such a loop is called a _____ loop.

a. 1990 Clean Air Act
b. Feedback
c. Feedback loop
d. Positive feedback

35. The _____ is a performance management tool for measuring whether the smaller-scale operational activities of a company are aligned with its larger-scale objectives in terms of vision and strategy.

By focusing not only on financial outcomes but also on the operational, marketing and developmental inputs to these, the _____ helps provide a more comprehensive view of a business, which in turn helps organizations act in their best long-term interests. This tool is also being used to address business response to climate change and greenhouse gas emissions.

a. Management development
b. Middle management
c. Commercial management
d. Balanced scorecard

36. A _____ is one of several ways of doing research whether it is social science related or even socially related. It is an intensive study of a single group, incident, or community.Other ways include experiments, surveys, multiple histories, and analysis of archival information .

Rather than using samples and following a rigid protocol to examine limited number of variables, _____ methods involve an in-depth, longitudinal examination of a single instance or event: a case.

a. Longitudinal study
b. Case study
c. 1990 Clean Air Act
d. Standard operating procedure

Chapter 1

1. b	2. c	3. d	4. a	5. d	6. b	7. b	8. a	9. d	10. b
11. d	12. d	13. d	14. a	15. c	16. d	17. a	18. d	19. d	20. d
21. a	22. c	23. d	24. b	25. d	26. d	27. c	28. d	29. c	30. c
31. d	32. a	33. c	34. a	35. d	36. d	37. c	38. d	39. a	40. b
41. d	42. a								

Chapter 2

1. d	2. a	3. c	4. c	5. a	6. a	7. d	8. a	9. a	10. a
11. d	12. a	13. a	14. c	15. b	16. d	17. d	18. d	19. b	20. b
21. d	22. d	23. d	24. d	25. a	26. a	27. b	28. d	29. b	30. a
31. a	32. d	33. d	34. a	35. a	36. c	37. a	38. d	39. a	40. d
41. d	42. c	43. d	44. b						

Chapter 3

1. d	2. b	3. d	4. a	5. c	6. c	7. d	8. d	9. b	10. d
11. b	12. d	13. d	14. c	15. d	16. c	17. c	18. d	19. c	20. a
21. d	22. d	23. b	24. c	25. d	26. d	27. a	28. b	29. a	30. d

Chapter 4

1. c	2. d	3. d	4. b	5. d	6. b	7. a	8. a	9. d	10. b
11. a	12. a	13. c	14. a	15. d	16. c	17. b	18. c	19. b	20. d
21. a	22. b	23. a	24. d	25. d					

Chapter 5

1. a	2. d	3. a	4. b	5. d	6. c	7. d	8. d	9. c	10. d
11. d	12. d	13. d	14. d						

Chapter 6

1. d	2. d	3. c	4. d	5. b	6. a	7. a	8. a	9. d	10. b
11. d	12. d	13. b	14. d	15. c	16. d	17. d	18. c	19. d	20. a
21. d	22. d	23. a	24. d	25. d	26. b	27. a	28. b	29. a	

Chapter 7

1. b	2. d	3. a	4. d	5. d	6. d	7. d	8. d	9. a	10. c
11. d	12. c	13. d	14. a	15. d	16. b	17. d	18. d	19. d	20. d
21. d	22. c	23. d	24. a	25. a	26. c	27. a	28. d	29. a	30. a
31. d	32. c	33. a	34. d	35. b	36. d	37. c	38. b	39. d	40. d
41. a	42. d	43. d	44. d	45. b	46. d	47. d			

Chapter 8

1. a	2. d	3. d	4. d	5. d	6. d	7. d	8. d	9. d	10. d
11. b	12. b	13. c	14. d	15. c	16. d	17. c	18. a	19. c	20. d
21. d	22. d	23. c	24. d	25. a					

ANSWER KEY

Chapter 9
1. d   2. a   3. a   4. b   5. c   6. a   7. d   8. b   9. d   10. d
11. a   12. c   13. d   14. b   15. d

Chapter 10
1. d   2. d   3. d   4. d   5. d   6. c   7. c   8. d   9. a   10. a
11. b   12. c   13. c   14. d   15. b   16. a   17. c   18. d   19. d

Chapter 11
1. d   2. d   3. d   4. c   5. d   6. c   7. d   8. d   9. c   10. a
11. c   12. b   13. d   14. a   15. d   16. d   17. d

Chapter 12
1. d   2. a   3. d   4. b   5. a   6. d   7. d   8. d   9. a   10. d
11. a   12. d   13. d   14. d

Chapter 13
1. a   2. b   3. b   4. b   5. c   6. d   7. d   8. d   9. d   10. d
11. b   12. c   13. c   14. b   15. c   16. d   17. d   18. b   19. c

Chapter 14
1. d   2. d   3. d   4. d   5. d   6. d   7. c   8. a   9. c   10. c
11. c   12. c   13. b   14. d   15. d   16. d   17. b   18. a   19. d   20. b
21. a   22. d   23. a   24. d   25. b   26. b   27. a   28. c   29. a   30. d
31. d   32. d   33. d   34. b   35. d   36. b

www.ingramcontent.com/pod-product-compliance
Lightning Source LLC
Chambersburg PA
CBHW082047230426
43670CB00016B/2805